THE DIALOG MASS

Midshipmen, U. S. Naval Academy, at Dialog Mass, Annapolis

THE DIALOG MASS

A Book for Priests and Teachers of Religion

BY

GERALD ELLARD, S.J., Ph.D.

PROFESSOR OF LITURGY IN ST. LOUIS UNIVERSITY,
AUTHOR OF "MEN AT WORK AT WORSHIP," ETC.

WITH A PREFACE BY

THE MOST REVEREND MICHAEL J. CURLEY, D.D.

ARCHBISHOP OF BALTIMORE AND WASHINGTON

LONGMANS, GREEN AND CO.

NEW YORK · TORONTO

1942

Imprimi potest

    P. A. BROOKS, S.J.
      Præpositus Provincialis
      Provinciae Missourianae, S.J.

St. Ludovici, die 31 Maii, 1941.

Nihil obstat

    ARTHUR J. SCANLAN, S.T.D.
      Censor Librorum

Imprimatur

    ✠FRANCIS J. SPELLMAN, D.D.
      Archbishop, New York

New York, March 5, 1942.

RAYMUNDO HENRICO MULLEN

SOCIETATIS IESU PRESBYTERO

CUNCTISQUE IN CHRISTI SACERDOTIO CONFRATRIBUS

QUO MAGIS NOS NOSTRAQUE SACRIFICIO CRUCIS CONFORMEMUR

QUO SALUBRIUS MYSTERIIS PLEBS SANCTA PARTICIPET

QUO ACTUOSIUS LITURGIAM FIDELES PERAGANT

EXIGUUM AMANTER LIBELLUM

DO DONO DEDICO

PREFACE

To those who have watched the progress of the Liturgical Movement in the United States these last few years it comes without surprise that the American hierarchy, through its corporate agency, the National Catholic Welfare Conference, will assume episcopal leadership of the Movement and integrate it into the ordinary framework of ecclesiastical affairs. This, too, is what has been done in other countries and was naturally to have been expected here; the particularly gratifying feature is that it is coming about much sooner than might have been thought some years ago. This move seems to give promise that the Catholic Church in the United States will not lag behind in gradually effecting that renewal and reform in corporate worship which the Holy See has so much at heart in our day.

The present book on what has come to be known as the *Missa Recitata,* or the Recited Mass, or, more simply, the Dialog Mass, points to the recent widespread recognition in this country of the place and function this form of Mass-worship occupies in the full program of the renewal of the Christian spirit through the active lay participation in the public offices of the Church. The ideal the Church here has in view, as is clear again and again in the papal directives, is the high Mass sung by priest, choir *and people.* Mother Church sees in the communal singing at her principal act of worship the ideal participation therein of the people in the pews. Both Pius X and Pius XI have spoken of it as being the primary and indispensable source of the true Christian spirit. But after generations in which the large body of the faithful have been but "mute and silent spectators," to use an expression of Pope Pius XI's, it is not easy to change at once into participation in song, and song, too, in a tongue that is not that of our daily lives.

Thus it is as a step towards this communal, or congregational, singing of high Mass, that Dialog Mass is conceived and introduced in first instance. I think it is particularly valuable that the author of this volume illustrates, at the end of the book, how unison recitation and responding at Dialog Mass, combined with a natural and appropriate use of song, provides a natural bridge to the more difficult, and more ideal, active lay participation in high Mass.

However Dialog Mass ought not be considered exclusively as a stepping-stone towards communal singing at high Mass. There will remain, as life is organized at present, a great many circumstances in which low Mass will be within the limitations of possibility, or convenience, or necessity, whereas high Mass will be beyond them. If the congregationally sung high Mass is the ideal type of high Mass, so also the congregational recitation and responding of the *Missa Recitata* will provide the ideal realization of the Eucharistic Sacrifice at what we call low Mass. The Church does not move violently in such matters, and she is patient in approaching her goal slowly and systematically. But it is well within the expectations of probability that another decade will have witnessed the gradual transition to Dialog Mass as the normal form of low Mass worship everywhere in the United States.

Some use of the *Missa Recitata,* as this volume brings out to one's surprise, is now being made in Sodality circles in fully one hundred dioceses of this country. Thus it is very valuable that we are at the outset provided with the historical background of the matter. The fully-documented account of the Holy See and the Dialog Mass, told here for the first time in English, and from sources not easily accessible in this country—that section of the book alone would be a worthwhile gift to his fellow-countrymen by the author.

Another surprise emerging from Father Ellard's study that may prove a little disconcerting to those living "in the heart of things" along the Atlantic seaboard, is that thus far the American leadership in this phase of the Church's worship reform has been in the Great Lakes and Upper Mississippi area. This is doubtless owing largely to the circumstance that the incipient Liturgical Movement in America has radiated from St. John's Abbey, Minnesota. In the matter of the introduction and spread of the Dialog Mass, which the Holy See has left entirely within the competence of the diocesan Ordinary, there has been up to now more immediate and far-reaching influence exerted in the regions named than at a greater distance. This is borne out, too, by a glance at the map in this volume, or at the statistical summary of the prevalence of Dialog Mass among the United States Sodalists.

Of a particularly convincing character are the two chapters detailing the results of official surveys on the present use of Dialog Mass in the Diocese of La Crosse and the Archdiocese of Chicago. In the former instance, in less than a decade, the Dialog Mass has won spontaneous adoption in more than half the parishes of the Diocese. The Catholic Youth Organization seems to have been the principal instrumentality relied upon in effecting this great change. In the metropolitan area of Chicago, in a movement that had begun before but which has been greatly accelerated under His Excellency Archbishop Stritch, one fourth of all the churches now use Dialog Mass.   The example set by the Archbishop of Chicago in sponsoring the first national Liturgical Week in 1940 now has its counterpart in his holding a summer school on Liturgy for priests at the great seminary at Mundelein.   We are informed that this three weeks' postgraduate school, so to speak, attracted priests from no less than thirty dioceses and ten religious orders.

From the standpoint of pastor and curate not the least valuable portions of this book, we believe, will be the final chapters.   We have already referred to one very pertinent feature embodied therein, the skillful combination of song with responding and recitation in such wise as to pave the way to congregational singing at high Mass and other services.   But sound and balanced and seasoned are the considerations advanced in connection with Dialog Mass both for youthful and adult congregations.   With his eyes not closed to the difficulties involved, but fixed calmly on the deep spiritual gains in this middle-phase of worship reform, Father Ellard charts a course that makes Dialog Mass seem inevitably the next step in the program of the Liturgical Movement in and for America.

Too long have our Mass-groups been mute and silent spectators.   At a time when social, economic and political bonds are breaking day after day, there is special timeliness in a work that knits minds and hearts together in the communal worship of our God.   May He prosper the Liturgical Movement in our midst, and may He deign in particular to bless the understanding and spread, according to the mind of the local Ordinary, of the *Missa Recitata!*

✠ MICHAEL J. CURLEY, D.D.,
Archbishop of Baltimore and Washington.

AUTHOR'S FOREWORD

In addressing a Priests' Liturgical Day, the first held
in the United States, His Excellency, the Most Reverend F. A. Thill of Concordia, stressed the special
propriety of such an observance in the very midst of
war: it was an example of putting first things first, he
was convinced. In similar fashion, the Most Reverend M. E. Kiley, Archbishop of Milwaukee, prescrib-
ing that the Sunday sermons of 1942 be given over
entirely to the liturgy, is persuaded of a special timeliness in such procedure. "Christ taught His Apos-
tles," he says, "to consecrate and entrusted to them the
administration of His Sacraments. . . . By His inspiration the Church has built around them a liturgy
so beautiful, so elevating, so consoling to the hearts
of her children as to make it, even from a purely hu-
man standpoint, the most powerful influence in the
world today." Like considerations weighed strongly
with His Excellency of Manchester, Most Reverend J.
B. Peterson, in introducing *The Proceedings of National Liturgical Week, 1941* to the public. "The
appearance of such a volume at this critical hour in
our history may be considered almost providential.
The battle now rages, physically as well as ideologically,
between Christian and anti-Christian forces. In its
final issue it may well be that the spiritual values represented in Catholic liturgy will have played no small
part in sustaining us, and in bringing us safely through
the valley of shadow to victory and peace in Christ
Jesus." [1] Immediately after the war had been carried

[1] *National Liturgical Week, 1941* (Newark: Benedictine Liturgical Conference, 1942), ix.

to our shores, the Catholic University of America, through its *Bulletin*,[2] assured American Catholics that it was putting the full weight of its position behind the liturgical movement in general, and made specific mention of its desire to foster the Dialog Mass. "The Catholic University of America would bear aloft the flaming torch, the expression of its motto, '*Deus Lux Mea*,' in the vanguard of the liturgical movement. . . . It would encourage, where feasible and with proper diocesan authorization, both the dialogue low Mass and the congregationally choral high Mass." Much similar action can be expected in authoritative circles, since the Sacred Congregation of the Council, by a special mandate of Pope Pius XII, as it states, has recently published a lengthy decree for bishops and pastors "immediately to teach the faithful concerning the nature and excellence of the Sacrifice of the Mass, . . . so that the faithful may not assist passively thereat." [3] One of the modes of *active* assistance in the holy Sacrifice, and the one that seems to be the 'bottle-neck' now preventing the realization of the full liturgical movement in this country, is dealt with in this volume, the so-called Dialog Mass.

Within a two-week period this spring the press carried accounts of the following items : As part of the social-planning convention of the Catholic Committee of the South, at Birmingham, April 21 and 22, the Most Reverend Bishops D. F. Desmond of Alexandria, and R. O. Gerow of Natchez, celebrated what has come to be known as Dialog Mass at the invitation of Bishop T. J. Toolen of Mobile. A few days later, Bishop J.

2 *The Catholic University Bulletin*, 9, 2 (December, 1941), "The Liturgy and the Laity," by W. J. Lallou, 8 *sqq.*
3 *American Ecclesiastical Review*, CVI, 1 (January, 1942), 36–39.

H. Schlarman of Peoria, as the guest of Bishop L. B. Kucera, preached before several thousands on Dialog Mass as a means of teaching Christian Doctrine at a Nebraska regional conference of the Confraternity of that name. Almost at the same time Bishop C. H. Winkelmann of Wichita had Bishop P. C. Schulte of Leavenworth celebrate Dialog Mass as part of the program of the Confraternity meeting in Kansas. A few days later, with Bishop Winkelmann preaching, Bishop Schulte celebrated Dialog Mass at the Kansas State Sodality Meet in Kansas City, Kansas; and, on the morrow Bishop E. V. O'Hara of Kansas City, Missouri, had a Dialog Mass demonstration by his Junior CYO as part of a Diocesan Eucharistic Congress. There can thus be little doubt that Dialog Mass is rapidly becoming a conspicuous feature of those extraordinary manifestations of Church life that attend congresses, conventions and giant demonstrations.

One might have noted also that *The Ecclesiastical Review* carried an article on "The Status of the '*Missa Recitata*'" in its May issue,[4] or that its companion journal, *The Homiletic and Pastoral Review* offered its readers in June an essay entitled "Presenting the 'Dialogue Mass.'"[5] That this same Dialog Mass, just now attracting nation-wide attention, may gain speedy entrance, and an understanding based on the mind of the local Ordinary, in more seminaries and religious houses, schools and institutions, and so gradually into more and more parish churches is the specific hope that has produced this little volume. It has been written in response to several requests and to supply a

[4] W. J. Lallou, *American Ecclesiastical Review*, CIV, 5 (May, 1941), 455.
[5] G. Zimpfer, *Homiletic and Pastoral Review*, XLI, 9 (June, 1941), 898-903.

need long felt in providing in not too inadequate fashion, we trust, the historical background of the matter. Here is presented for the first time in our language, as far as one knows, the full story of Pope Pius XI and Dialog Mass. Nor in any single source known to me could one follow the trend of the ordinary *magisterium* of the Church Universal by perusing multiple enactments of national and local councils, synods, bishops' pastorals, sermons, authoritative pronouncements. Against that more or less ecumenical backdrop are presented three dioramas, so to speak, of Dialog Mass in our own country. In the first of these there march the results of a private but nation-wide survey made by the Sodality of the Blessed Virgin: this section is enhanced and enriched by the written statements of some two-score American archbishops and bishops. The second diorama affords a parish-by-parish glimpse, touching Dialog Mass, in the Diocese of La Crosse, again with statements by the Most Reverend Ordinary and Auxiliary. An official and complete 'census' of Dialog Mass in all the churches and chapels of the Archdiocese of Chicago, undertaken by the directions of Most Reverend S. A. Stritch, next unfolds before the reader. Separate sections at the end group studies and suggestions on Dialog Mass for children, where the relation of this mode of Mass-Worship to music is studied, and on the different attitudes necessitated by a predominantly adult congregation. Thus is sought to provide a handy manual not lacking any element needed for the historical, canonical, pastoral and practical study of what the Sacred Congregation of Rites has termed "this praiseworthy mode" of Mass-attendance.

The relation of this small volume to two preceding ones by the same author will doubtless be a question asked by his former readers. In *Christian Life and Worship,* addressed in first instance to the collegiate students, are studied the principles of Catholic corporate worship in the entire field of Sacrifice, Sacraments and Sacramentals, Corporate Prayer. One chapter only in that volume dealt with the Liturgical Movement. That chapter was extended to book-length in *Men at Work at Worship* and presented to the consideration of the vastly wider group of adult Catholics of all mature ages and 'classes.' In that second work one chapter dealt with Dialog Mass. For the thousands of priests and Catholic educators in the United States an ampler handling of that same subject-matter is herewith presented. Thus the three books are as three stories of a building, and that a few cardinal quotations reappear in each is no more surprising than that structural lines carry through from foundation to roof. But unless the Lord build the house they labor in vain that build it, and so it is with the prayer that the Divine Artificer fashion and form this portion of His temple amongst us that the booklet is committed to the light.

Small as it is, this book bears the impress of many services done the author. By its statistical character it could not have been compiled without the help of hands in many places. The Most Reverend Apostolic Delegate in our midst saw fit to foster and enrich the volume. The Cardinal Primates of both England and Ireland took the time and trouble to write on its behalf. So did many members of our own hierarchy in all parts of the country, and in particular their gracious Excellencies of Chicago, La Crosse and Baltimore-Washington. The undertaking was both encouraged by my superiors and materially aided by my religious brethren, those of *The Queen's Work* staff in first instance. The book's unusual typographical demands were a continuous challenge to the skill of the publishers, and have, I believe, resulted in a triumph of expert artistry. Some chapters that had appeared in *The Journal of Religious Instruction* are thence reprinted with permission, as likewise a passage from *The Review For Religious*. God further blessing it, may the book assist, in an historic hour, millions of our countrymen towards a more abundant use of the inexhaustible riches of the Eucharist, towards an 'all-out' Mass for the life of the world.

GERALD ELLARD, S.J., Ph.D.

St. Mary's College, St. Marys, Kansas,
Feast of St. Gregory the Great, March 12, 1942.

CONTENTS

ILLUSTRATIONS

THE DIALOG MASS

CHAPTER I

THE DIALOG MASS IN THE LITURGICAL MOVEMENT

In reading the history of the papacy one is struck again and again by the suggestion that pontiffs inaugurate programs, the ulterior results of which, however dimly glimpsed beforehand by their promoters, become evident in substance only at a much later date. And it is in no sense derogatory to the papal office to suggest that the Vicars of Christ did not at the time see the consequences for good as well as for evil that later emerged from their policies. Thus, to go no farther back than the Social Movement of Pope Leo XIII : it must be evident to any thinking man that we, in the central decades of this century, see depths of meaning unsuspected by Pope Leo himself in those words written at the time of his death. "Catholic Action," wrote an ambassador to the Vatican in 1903, as Leo lay on his catafalque, "has been oriented for long years, perhaps for centuries, in the direction given it by the great pope who has just disappeared. . . Such action, intellectual at other times, and 'political' in yet others, will today be social." [1]

And when Pope Pius X took those steps that officially inaugurated the reform of worship we call the Litur-

[1] E. Soderini, *The Pontificate of Pope Leo XIII*, (London: Burns, Oates and Washbourne, Ltd., 1935), I, 223.

1

gical Movement, he might have been greatly surprised
if he had been told that he was giving occasion and
impetus to a form of liturgical piety now universally
known as the Dialog Mass.   One might apply to this
small detail words that Pius X used in connection with
his efforts towards the reform of the Roman breviary.
Middle-aged and elderly priests will recall that there
was a revision of the breviary during that pontificate.
The revisions, such as they were, centering around the
distribution of the psalms over the entire week, and
the restoration to use of the Sunday Masses and Offices,
were but an initial step towards the goal he had in
view.   The ultimate objective of thorough-going reform, especially on the historical side, was dependent
upon patient scholarship over a long period.   "But
all these [reform projects]," wrote Pius in publishing
his *ad interim* revisions, "demand in the judgment of
learned and prudent men, studies both difficult and
protracted.   Hence, a cycle of many years must elapse
before the liturgical temple, so to speak, which the mystical Bride of Christ fashioned with cunning skill to
portray her love and faith, stands forth once more in
its dignity and beauty, after the disfigurement of age
has been cleansed away (*deterso squalore vetustatis*)." [2]
A phase of the beauty and dignity of the temple that
was perhaps entirely unsuspected by Pius X himself
emerges now as the Dialog Mass.   Just what is meant
by this expression, and what is the relationship of the
Dialog Mass to the Liturgical Movement as a whole?
In the Dialog Mass the entire congregation answers,
along with its official representative, the server, to the
priest, in running dialog, and recites, along with its

---

[2] *Abhinc duos annos*, Motu proprio, Oct. 13, 1913: cf. *American Ecclesiastical Review*, Vol. L, 1 (January, 1914), 54 *sqq.*

hierarchical officiant, the priest, some of the parts sung at a high Mass, such as the *Gloria* and *Credo*.

The case for the Dialog Mass as part of the Liturgical Movement might be stated syllogistically as follows :

The Liturgical Movement seeks to restore active lay participation in Catholic public worship.

But the Dialog Mass affords active lay participation in Catholic public worship.

Therefore, the Liturgical Movement embodies the Dialog Mass as a means to its end.

But the very fact that I speak of a "case" for the Dialog Mass, or appeal to a syllogism to give it footing, indicates that it is an accretion to the Liturgical Movement as originally inaugurated. If for the sake of argument we say that the modern Liturgical Movement rests chiefly on Pius X's first great *Motu proprio* on sacred music of November 22, 1903, it is clear that the Supreme Pontiff was legislating for active lay participation by means of singing the high Mass chants. Thus, the active lay participation by means of responding and reciting low Mass prayers is active participation in a different sphere, and, as things stand now, an incomparably wider sphere. And if we suggest that the Dialog Mass was doubtless an unforeseen development of the wished-for lay participation, this is because the Holy See has never enjoined Dialog Mass, and, as will be set out in detail later, took an attitude of reserve and caution towards it for some years. It was not until 1935 that it became perfectly clear that the Holy See had no objection to the introduction and supervision of the Dialog Mass by the local Ordinary in every diocese.

Again, if we ask for the special timeliness just now

in having educators in America acquaint themselves with the concepts, the history and the initial procedures in introducing the Dialog Mass, the reason could be stated as follows:

> On the one hand, American Catholics are now fairly well converted to the use of the missal, a prerequisite for most forms of active lay participation.
>
> On the other hand, barring notable local exceptions, the country as a whole, seems to be about as far from the prescribed form of active participation at high Mass as it was four decades ago. Therefore, the easy, introductory and intermediate method of active lay participation in low Mass, besides being a great good in itself, is the psychological and the logical step towards that form of worship set out in the papal prescriptions.

To foster it would seem to be one of the most effective ways of following the true mind of our mother, the Church.

Let us go into the matter in somewhat greater detail. First of all we are confronted with the basic question of active lay participation in *Catholic* worship. It has been objected over and over against modern Catholic worship that lay worshippers, despite their orthodoxy, suffer these three enormous handicaps:

(1) They are cut off from participation through hearing by the use of an unknown language.

(2) They are cut off from participation through singing by the use of music too difficult for the people.

(3) They are cut off from communal, if silent, par-

ticipation by reason of the absence of a manual, and the widespread ignorance of the meaning of the ritual acts.

The service of God in public worship, as elsewhere, is a reasonable service. It is not without a deep, psychological significance that every group that has broken away from Catholic unity in modern times has disengaged itself from the incubus of these handicaps. "Let them all sing, and they will all become Lutherans," was an oft-repeated sixteenth-century slogan : it is pathetic in the extreme to see how millions were tricked into unorthodoxy when they thought they were being admitted into active lay participation for which they yearned.

It must be clear that such a situation is abnormal, is not what divine wisdom intended Christian public worship to be, is a phase of Church-life demanding revision, reform.   St. Paul wanted the layman to be in a position, by reason of having understood the public prayer to "say the *Amen* to thy thanksgiving" (I Cor. xiv, 16).   He wanted the Ephesian Christians to be "speaking one to another in psalms and hymns and spiritual songs" (Eph. v, 19).   While Paul himself enjoyed that miraculous gift of tongues, whereby he was able to proclaim the wondrous works of God even in languages he himself did not understand, and enjoyed it more than all his Corinthian converts, and thanked God for it, "nevertheless in church I had rather speak five words with my understanding, so as to instruct others, than ten thousand words 'in a tongue'" (I Cor. xiv, 19).   And as for purely volitional association with public prayers he did not understand, that was unsuited, he felt, for Christian assemblies, where the neighbor is to be *built up* (edified) :

"For if I pray in a 'tongue,' my spirit prayeth, but
my understanding reapeth no fruit.

What then is [to be done?]

I will pray with my spirit,

I will pray with my understanding also:

I will sing with my spirit,

I will sing with my understanding also.

Else, if thou bless [God] in spirit [alone], how
shall he that filleth the place of the layman
say the *Amen* to thy thanksgiving?

For he knoweth not what thou sayest: thy
thanksgiving is no doubt good, but thy neighbor is not edified."

(I Cor. xiv, 14-17)

So taught St. Paul, despite the fact that he knew as
well as any theologians since his time that the essence
of Catholic worship is what *Christ* does therein, and
that the essence is saved even if the by-standers (or
even the priest) know very little about what is being
done.   The fruits and values of the worship *ex opere
operato Christi* are won, even if the *other* worshippers
take no part *ex opere operantium* in the rites that ex-
ternalize Christ's ACTION.

Yet how abnormal the situation of lay-exclusion (by
the very force of circumstances) from any corporate
participation, or even intelligent private participation,
really was, or is, becomes clear if we but confront that
principle on which Pius X grounded his reform.   His
words, until they shall have become second nature to
Catholics, cannot be quoted too often:

"Filled as we are with a most ardent desire to see the
true Christian spirit * flourish in every respect and be
preserved by all the faithful, we deem it necessary to

* Italics ours.

provide before aught else for the sanctity and dignity of the temple, in which the faithful assemble for no other object than of *acquiring this spirit* * from its foremost and indispensable font, *which is the active participation* * in the most holy mysteries and in the public and solemn prayers of the Church." [3]

To this end everything else must yield : to this end "Endeavor should be made as far as possible to restore Gregorian plainsong *to the use* of the people, so that *the faithful may again take a more active part in the ecclesiastical offices, as was the case in ancient times.*" [4]*

For the sake of the full picture, be it stated very clearly at this point that the reforms inaugurated by Pope Pius X were planned, even to details, long before his time, as far back, indeed, as the Council of Trent in the sixteenth century. A subsequent section will deal directly with that fact, and will serve to indicate the adverse circumstances which resulted in the postponement of this phase of the Tridentine reform until our own age.

When Pius X, then, put his hand to the task so long planned and so long delayed, of reforming Catholic worship, he set down his guiding principle in the words we have just quoted at length. It is not a question of reform for the sake of reform, not a question of this type of music or of that for reasons of art or beauty (though these come in incidentally), it is not a question of this or that particular action of lay participation for the sake of dignity or seemliness, but it is

* Italics ours.
[3] *Motu Proprio, On Sacred Music*, Nov. 22, 1903: translation, *Catholic Church Music*, (London: Burns, Oates and Washbourne, Ltd.), 1933, 3.
[4] *Op. cit.*, 23, cf. 5, translation cited as from Letter of Cardinal Vicar, the original being the same.

active participation because that was held to be a foremost and indispensable font of the true Christian spirit, so inescapably necessary for the sanctification of the twentieth century.

With this principle clearly in view, and carrying out (we again insist) plans long matured and held in reserve for the right moment, Pius X proceeded to foster active lay participation on the part of all in these three manners :

(1) By making it *possible,* and *obligatory,* for them to sing at high Mass.   This program was begun in 1903, and enjoined repeatedly.

(2) By making it *possible,* and *laudable,* for them to receive Holy Communion frequently, even daily, if free from known mortal sins.

(3) By making it *laudable,* and to some extent obligatory in *Rome,* for the laity to have the missal prayers.

The second item on this program marked a sweeping change in Catholic pastoral practice against the usage of centuries.   The matter at issue, of course, was disciplinary, but it touched Catholic piety at its very core.   No papal decree for centuries was greeted with more marked tokens of gratitude ; just as it is equally true to say that no decree in our century has been more widely resisted and evaded than the one on congregational singing of the plainsong.   The one and the other look to the same end, popular participation in public worship in two different manners !

The last item on the program is little known and requires a word of elucidation.   In Jansenist times there had taken place, against Roman legislation, it is true, but nevertheless actually and over a wide area (the whole of France was at one time involved, and other countries were also infected), what we might call the abandonment of the Roman liturgical books, and the substitution of rites locally composed. As long as the new books remained in Latin, the faith of the common people would not readily be contaminated by them. When the subsequent project of rendering them into the vernacular was broached, Rome reacted with sternness and vigor : it was made a matter of excommunication to publish missals in the vernacular. With the gradual waning of the danger, the prohibition had lost its point : Pius IX mitigated it, Leo XIII withdrew it entirely. Pius X, in publishing a revision of the catechism to be used in Rome, added for his diocesan subjects prayers recommended for use on Sundays at the Eucharistic Sacrifice. These prayers are the Ordinary and Canon of the Mass, what we call today a leaflet missal minus the proper of the day.

In the same catechism, as revised and published for Rome by Pius X, there is a passage on what we might call the supernatural psychology of the Church Year. It touches intimately the matter here discussed, active lay participation in Catholic public worship :

"The feasts were instituted for the very purpose of rendering a common supreme cult of adoration to God in His temples. The ceremonies, words, melodies, in a word, all the externals, have been so well assembled and adapted to diverse circumstances that the mysteries and the truths of the events celebrated cannot but penetrate into the soul and there produce the corresponding acts and sentiments. If the faithful were well-instructed, and celebrated the feasts in the spirit intended by the Church when she instituted them, there would be a notable renewal and increase of faith, piety and religious instruction; the entire life of the Christian would thereby become better and stronger." [5]

Every good Christian by knowledge and encouragement would be led into a more active participation, with a consequent betterment of the entire Christian life.

Pius X's provisions for the restoration of plainchant were considered in 1903 to be "so clear as to need no special dilucidation," but that hope being dashed, the Cardinal Vicar of Rome restated and reinforced them in 1912. Prefatory remarks over, his statement begins as follows:

"The best ecclesiastical traditions demand that the whole assembly of the faithful should join in the singing at all liturgical functions, by executing the parts of the text which are assigned to the choir, and that a special *Schola Cantorum* should alternate with the people, undertaking the more richly melodious parts, which should be strictly reserved to them. For this reason our Holy Father in his venerable *Motu proprio* of November 22, 1903, prescribed as follows: (par. 3), 'Endeavor should be made as far as possible to restore the Gregorian plainchant to the use of the people, in order that the faithful may once again take a more active part in ecclesiastical functions, as was the custom in olden times.'" [6]

Farther on this letter becomes more specific as to what constitutes the people's part, when it urges pastors, by explaining the "high aims of the Holy Father," and inviting "the faithful to cooperate in this matter especially by taking a more active part in the sacred

---

[5] Quoted here at second hand from L. Beauduin-V. Michel, *Liturgy, The Life of the Church,* (Collegeville, Minn.: The Liturgical Press, 1926), 34.

[6] Letter of Cardinal Vicar, Feb. 2, 1912: translation quoted from *Catholic Church Music,* (London: Burns, Oates and Washbourne, Ltd.), 1933, 22, 23.

functions, in singing the *Kyrie Eleison,* the *Gloria,* etc., at high Mass, as well as in the psalms, the more familiar liturgical hymns, and hymns in the vulgar tongue." [7]   In fine, no effort was to be spared to effect that the entire congregation "may join in the parts allotted to the people." [8]

So spoke Pius X at the beginning, the middle and end of his pontificate.   Documents before me, dealing with this subject from one angle or another, bear dates of 1903, 1905, 1906, 1908, 1910, 1912, and 1913.   For him active lay participation would be the result of knowledge, and would consist, besides using a missal, in the reception of Communion and in singing congregationally the Church's song.

Pope Benedict XV, for all the demands of the former World War upon his time, praised and blessed endeavors afoot to hold a Liturgical Congress "for the purpose of promoting a salutary reawakening of faith and of Christian piety."   He said in part :

"For the spread amongst the faithful of an exact acquaintance with the liturgy : to inspire in their hearts a holy delight in the prayers, rites and chant, by means of which, in union with their common Mother, they pay their worship to God ; to attract them to take an active part in the sacred Mysteries and in the ecclesiastical festivals : — All this cannot but serve admirably to bring the faithful into closer union with the priest, to lead them back to the Church, to nourish their piety, to give renewed vigor to their faith, to better their lives" . . . [9]

This document neither includes nor excludes the

[7] *Op. cit.,* paragraph 16.
[8] *Op. cit.,* paragraph 17.
[9] Letter to Rt. Rev. Marcet, O.S.B. (Montserrat), March 15, 1915: original published in *Vida Christiana,* 1 (1914-15), p. 247: translation in *Orate Fratres,* Vol. IX, 7 (May 18, 1935), 325.

type of active participation which consists in responding and reciting at low Mass, what we call the Dialog
Mass. That was, in all likelihood, still unknown at
Rome, although by that date, 1915, it was making its
appearance in the north.

When the *solicitudo omnium ecclesiarum* descended
on the shoulders of Pius XI, it lacked little of a quarter
century since the *Motu proprio* of Pius X. That an-
niversary was not to be allowed to pass unnoticed,
especially as it coincided with the sacerdotal golden
jubilee of Pius XI. The new pontiff issued an Apostolic Constitution, *On Divine Worship,* vigorously and
clearly restating the end and the means of the papal
program of worship reform. In the short quotation
that follows none will fail to note the old ideas, or the
quickened tempo of the Post-War Vatican :

"In our times the chief object of Pope Pius X, in the
Motu proprio which he issued twenty-five years ago,
making certain prescriptions concerning Gregorian
Chant and sacred music, was *to arouse and foster a
Christian spirit in the faithful** ... The faithful come
to church in order to derive piety from its chief source
by taking an active part in the venerated mysteries and
in the public solemn prayers of the Church." [10]

Once the principles on which music is admitted into
the service of worship have been rapidly discussed, the
Vicar of Christ reverts again to the same theme of
active lay participation. The quotation is somewhat
lengthy, but in the whole matter of the Liturgical
Movement is of the highest importance :

"In order that the faithful may more actively participate in divine worship, let them be made once more

[10] Pius XI, *On Divine Worship,* Dec. 20, 1928: *Acta Apostolicae Sedis,*
XXI (1929), 33 *sqq.*
* Italics ours.

to sing the Gregorian Chant, as far as it belongs to them to take part in it. It is most important that when the people assist in the sacred ceremonies, or when pious sodalities take part with the clergy in a procession, they should not be merely detached and silent spectators, but, filled with a deep sense of the beauty of the liturgy, they should sing alternately with the clergy or the choir, as it is prescribed. If this is done, then it will no longer happen that the people either make no answer at all to the public prayers — whether in the language of the liturgy or in the ver- nacular — or at best utter the responses in a low and subdued murmur." [11]

It will be noted that in this last sentence, Pius XI says the communal singing will react upon and revivify communal responding at public prayers : the modern Dialog Mass begins at the other, and easier end, and by stimulating community consciousness by respond- ing and reciting at low Mass, leads the way to congre- gational singing at high Mass and other functions.

The rubrics of the solemn pontifical Mass prescribe that the canons and the vested ministers in the sanc- tuary, whose number may run into dozens, should re- cite two by two the prayers said at the foot of the altar and the *Kyrie,* and that all together should recite in unison with the bishop celebrant the *Gloria, Credo, Sanctus-Benedictus.*[12] This is, so to speak, a clerical Dialog Mass sandwiched into a high Mass. Our next chapter will deal with active lay participation in Chris- tian antiquity and the middle ages, of which this cler- ical "Dialog Mass" at the Bishop's high Mass is some- thing of a miniature.

[11] *Ibid.,* paragraph 43 : *Catholic Church Music,* § IX, 43.
[12] *Caeremoniale Episcoporum,* II, viii, 32, 36, 39, 52.

CHAPTER II

ACTIVE PARTICIPATION AND TRADITION

"The Flemings frequent their churches zealously, but very early in the mornings. The priests are quite slow in saying their Masses, in which they differ a good deal from Italians, and they say them so low that no one hears their voices. They do not permit anyone to make the responses, except the servers, and no one else." So wrote Canon Antonio de Beatis, Secretary to Cardinal Louis of Aragon, of a trip to Flanders in 1518.[1] At the papal court at that time, as we chance to know from one of its famous masters of ceremonies, it was the custom for all bystanders, even the Supreme Pontiff, when he was present, to make the responses to a priest celebrating low Mass. Nor would the Canon have made this observation had not the exclusion of the worshippers, the servers excepted, from making the responses struck him as a novelty. Does this imply that the Dialog Mass, as we know it now, is something very old in the Church? No, it does not: not, that is, without an important distinction between substance and manner. The substance, or what we call active participation by the lay worshippers in holy Mass, is as old as the Mass itself. The procedure now known as Dialog Mass, whereby the entire congregation joins in making the short responses and joins with the priest

[1] Quoted by G. Lefebvre in "Les Questions de la Messe Dialoguée," *La Participation Active des Fidèles au Culte* (Louvain: Mont-César, 1934), 176-177 from *Le Correspondant* (March 10, 1913), 1017.

in reciting certain portions that are sung at high Mass, this is in part the old restored, in part the new adapted and adopted. The present chapter proposes to survey in cursory fashion the tradition throughout the centuries of active lay participation in the Mass of the Roman Rite.

But first let us set down, as guiding beacons for our considerations, two facts of inestimable importance in such a study. The first of these guiding ideas is this: The earliest Mass that leaves a recorded history is in the most elaborate form of all, what we call the solemn pontifical Mass. At this Mass the Bishop was, as now, surrounded by his clergy of all ranks, high and low, but in addition to this, what is no longer the case, he was joined by them all in the sacramental *concelebration* of the Eucharistic Mysteries. Thus, the numerous clerical assistants had not only auxiliary ceremonial functions in the composite rite, but all of them, in their own order, actually concelebrated the one Mass. Each one in priest's orders, for instance, was concelebrant with the bishop and the other priests. Newly ordained priests still do this in their ordination Mass. The prescription of the *Caeremoniale Episcoporum* that all vested ministers in the sanctuary, and all canons in choir (also in the sanctuary), at pontifical high Mass are to recite two by two the prayers at the foot of the altar, and are to recite in unison with the officiating prelate the *Gloria, Credo* and *Sanctus,* is still a vivid reminder of the old concelebration. This solemn pontifical Mass, moreover, demanded a wide range of assistants, priests, archdeacons, deacons, subdeacons, lectors, acolytes, cantors, two choirs on opposite sides of the sanctuary, and the rest of the congregation. The principle of the "division of functions," so to speak, was carried out so consistently that the celebrant's manual, for instance, did not even contain the lessons or choral parts, as not belonging to the officiant.

Alongside this Mass, celebrated with what we might call a full complement of auxiliary participants, there was for necessity in outlying places, a type of Mass that resembles our *Missa Cantata*. In this the celebrant "took over" the functions of lector and deacon to chant the lessons in their absence. The people sang the short responses. In this Mass, historians think, there were no "proper" choral parts. About the Gradual we are not clearly informed, but Introit, Offertory and Communion anthems, were then, it would seem, considered special features of the papal or episcopal Masses.[2]

The second all-important fact by which to chart our reflections is this : It is not known when low Mass began to be celebrated. From a careful consideration of all the early evidence now known it is possible to say with certainty that there was, from time to time and by way of exception, Mass in a private dwelling, or in the presence of a few people only, but it is not possible to say if these "private" Masses were not sung or chanted by celebrant, lector and assistants, in much the same manner as the customary "public" Masses. This much is certain : low Mass, in our sense of the term, was from the sixth century on becoming constantly commoner, and by the eighth century it was known everywhere. It would seem to have been the "normal" form of the Mass of the Roman Rite, in con-

---

[2] L. Eisenhofer, *Handbuch der Katholischen Liturgik* (Freiburg: Herder, 1933), II, 9: "Wer das *Graduale* sang, wird nicht gesacht . . . Die Wechselgesänge, *Introitus, Offertorium, Communio,* ebenso anfangs auch das *Agnus Dei* waren wahrscheinlich zunächst nur eine Eigentümlichkeit der päpstlichen oder bischöflichen Messe."

tradistinction to the old Celtic Rite, the old Gallican Rite, and so forth, on the emergence of Christendom after the breakup of the Empire.

If there is a third factor of almost equal moment in the historical conditioning of our mode of worship it would be the use of the vernacular. As long as the Church was spreading among peoples that had a written language, the Church in both East and West quite naturally took that language for its offices of public worship. A fixed, or written, native language was necessary, because the Gospel-story, for instance, and the sacramental forms, are "fixed," but once such a language was at hand the necessity of active lay participation dictated that the prayers and chants of the Church be in the language the people understood.[3] As late as 800, as there is abundant evidence to prove, in all that area that had been part of the Roman Empire of the West, the people, however unlettered, heard and understood from altar and choir the language they used at home and fireside. Just so an illiterate of today can follow the faultless form that should characterize a public address, even though he know nothing of the grammarian's rules observed in its composition. It was not until the medieval period that language was a barrier to active lay participation in Catholic worship. In fact, since even elementary schooling was imparted in Latin, and since the texts used for reading and singing were liturgical texts, it is true only of those who had no schooling whatsoever to say that they could not understand in some degree or join in singing

[3] J. A. Jungmann, *Die Liturgische Feier: Grundsätzliches und Geschichtliches über Formgesetze der Liturgie* (Regensburg: Pustet, 1939), 49-53. This work has now appeared as *Liturgical Worship: A Historical Inquiry Into Its Fundamental Principles*, translated by a monk [Rev. Otto Eisenzimmer] of St. John's Abbey (New York: Pustet, 1941); cf. 56-64.

the Latin of altar and choir.   Pope Pius XI was thinking of what we may call the cathedral-building period
of the Middle Ages when he wrote in *On Divine Worship* : "It was in the churches, finally, where practically
the whole city formed a great joint choir, that the
workers, builders, artists, sculptors and writers gained
from the liturgy that deep knowledge of theology
which is now so apparent in the monuments of the
Middle Ages." [4]   But, since the Renaissance, it is only
in Italy, I dare say, that the wall between vernacular
and Latin is so thin as to be penetrable by the people
as a group.

By way of presenting a comprehensive picture in a
single frame, it is proposed here to put into tabular
form the various modes of active lay participation in
holy Mass, with an indication of how these have been
present at four distinct periods of the Church's long
lifetime, namely, the primitive age, the patristic, the
medieval-and-modern, and, finally, as in the program
of the liturgical reforms inaugurated by Pius X.
After presenting the table, comment on individual
items will be in place. The table follows :

With this table before us, one might offer a few
wide generalizations. One will note, first, that between the primitive and the end of the patristic period,
while retaining practically everything that had been
received from the beginning, there was a large development in the sphere of lay participation.

A. Participation in the new choral elements, as they
were added, the Gradual alone excepted. The
people's singing of the *Gloria Patri* at the end of
the Introit-Psalm was a compensation that came

[4] Pius XI, "On Divine Worship," *Divini Cultus Sanctitatem,* 1928, AAS
XXI, 34.

ACTIVE LAY PARTICIPATION IN HOLY MASS

Mode of Participation	Primitive	Patristic (to 600)	Medieval-Modern	Twentieth Century
1. Processional entrance	For all: vernacular	For all (on occasions)	In Latin. For all, but dying out	For all: in Latin, restoration urged
2. Singing responses		For all: vernacular		For all: in Latin, restoration urged
3. Singing choral parts	For all: "psalms, hymns, canticles," (Col. iii, 16)	For all: *Gloria Patri* (Int.) *Kyrie* *Sanctus*	For all: in Latin, dying out *Kyrie* *Gloria in Excelsis* *Sequentia* *Credo* *Sanctus* *Agnus Dei*	For all: in Latin, restoration urged *Kyrie* *Gloria in Excelsis* *Credo* *Sanctus* *Agnus Dei*
4. Hearing Scripture lessons	In vernacular	In vernacular	In Latin	In Latin
5. "Bede"—Prayers after Gospel			In vernacular (Med.)	
6. Offertory Anthem* and Procession		For all (by sexes)		
7. Postures, standing, etc.	Same as clergy	Same as clergy	"Lay" postures only	"Lay" postures only
8. Kiss of Peace	For all (by sexes)	For all (by sexes)		
9. Sacramental Communion	For all	For many	For few only	For all (urged)
10. Communion Anthem* and Procession		For Communicants (by sexes)		
11. Fasting Attendance		For all present	for Communicants only	for Communicants only
12. Receiving Blessed Bread after Mass			For all (Med.)	
13. Reciting low Mass responses			For by-standers	For all (Dialog Mass)
14. Reciting at low Mass, *Gloria, Credo, Sanctus, Agnus Dei*				For all (Dialog Mass)

* People sang fixed verse, alternately with choir, chanting psalm.

in when the adoption of responsorial chant had
made the people's former participation in the
psalmody, by means of a recurring "chorus," no
longer possible.[5]

B. Personal participation in the essential symbol-
ism of the sacrificial rite by the contribution of a
gift personally presented.

C. Participation by action in marching in group
formation : to the church for Mass ; to the altar
for the gift-giving at the Offertory ; to the altar
for the Gift-Getting at the Communion. All the
processions were accompanied by singing.

In the long period, 600-1900, for multiple reasons
that need not be dealt with here, there was a notable
decline in lay participation in the celebration of holy
Mass. Most regrettable was the falling off in the reception of sacramental Communion, always an integral
part of sacrificial worship. Again, processional participation disappeared as a regular feature of Mass
worship. The kiss of peace, and other worship ges-
tures and postures previously shared alike with the
clergy, little by little became "clerical." [6] Choral
parts did continue to multiply, and insofar offered
fresh scope for congregational song. But when the
music became too difficult for congregational use all
but a few were forced into silence. But that the spirit
of active participation was seeking new ways in which
to express itself, was searching for substitutes, so to
speak, for old and vanished forms of active participa-

[5] J. A. Jungmann, *Die Liturgische Feier*, 78, 79.
[6] This seems a suitable place to call attention to a seldom-mentioned
form of lay participation at Mass in patristic times, that the entire congregation should be fasting. The late Herbert Thurston has an illuminating
article on the subject, "Your Sacrifice and Mine," *American Ecclesiastical
Review*, xci (1934), 565-577.

tion, became manifest again and again. Among these passing medieval substitutes for older ways we have signalized the recitation, after the Gospel, of prayers in the vernacular for urgent needs, since the prayers in the official language were no longer understood, and the reception of "blessed bread" by all after Mass, as a quasi-substitute for sacramental Communion, now became a thing of great rarity.

A rapid glance at the last column to the right of the table shows that the liturgical reform inaugurated by Pope Pius X began with the hoped-for restoration of congregational singing in all the people's traditional parts of the song, and the restoration of integral sacrificial worship for the laity by the reception of Communion "frequently, even daily." In the Dialog Mass there is continued and enlarged a former practice of congregational responding to the priest. In the unbroken spirit of the Christian worship from the beginning, there has been introduced one new mode of active participation suited to our age, the unison recitation with the celebrant of the *Gloria, Credo, Sanctus* and *Agnus Dei*. Now to engage some factors at closer range.

It is difficult to know just what to select in documenting this table. Two general descriptions of Mass are given first, one reflecting general conditions as St. John Chrysostom knew them in the East about 400, the second reprehending a scandalous state of affairs St. Cæsarius of Arles had encountered in southern Gaul just about a hundred years later. Both citations are of some length, but all the richer in instructive detail. Chrysostom is explaining that honor done to a messenger of the Church passes to the body of the faithful, and "great is the power of that assembly."

"Certain it is at least that the prayer of the Church loosed Peter from his chains, opened the mouth of Paul; their voice also in no slight degree arms those that arrive at spiritual rule. . .

"But there are occasions on which there is no advantage to the priest over those under him; for instance, when we are about to partake of the awful Mysteries. For we are all alike counted worthy of the same things: not as under the Old Testament, [when] the priest partook of some foods and those under him of others, and it was not lawful for the people to eat of those things whereof the priest partook. Not so now, before all one Body is set and one Cup.

"And in the prayers also one may observe the people making their own important contribution. For on behalf of those possessed, on behalf of those doing penance, our prayers are made in common, both by priest and people, and all say the same prayer, a prayer replete with pity.

"Again, when [at the dismissal of the catechumens] we have excluded from the holy precincts those unable as yet to partake of the Holy Table, how fitting that another prayer is offered, and we all alike fall prostrate, and all together rise again. Again, when it is time to give and to receive the [kiss of] peace, we all alike salute each other.

"Again, in the most awful Mysteries themselves, the priest prays for the people, and the people in turn pray for the priest; for the words, *with thy spirit*, are nothing else than this. The offering of the Eucharist again is common; for neither doth he [the priest] give thanks alone, but all the people do the same. He first enlists their voices, and only when they assent that it is 'meet and right to do so,' does he begin the Eucharistic prayer. And do you wonder that the people speak with the priest, when with the very Cherubim and Powers above they jointly sing those sacred hymns?" [7]

Listen, now, to the shocked expressions of St. Cæsarius, who had chanced upon a congregation that, for the most part, left the church after the sermon. How, he wants to know, can the Mass be celebrated without them?

"If you pay diligent attention [St. Cæsarius instructs them] you will see that the Mass does not consist in the recitation of the Scriptural lessons in the church, but in the offering of the gifts and in the consecration of the Body and Blood of the Lord. For, as for the lessons, whether they be from the prophets or epistles or the gospels, you can either read them yourselves or hear others read in your own homes, but the consecration of the Body of the Lord you can neither hear nor witness anywhere but in the house of God.

"Therefore, he that wishes to celebrate Mass completely to the profit of his own soul, must remain in the church with lowly posture of body and compunction of heart until the *Pater Noster* is said and the blessing given to the people. For when the greater part of the congregation — nay, what is worse, nearly the whole — leave the church after the lessons have been read, who is there to whom the priest can address his *Sursum Corda* [lift up your hearts]? Or how can those say they have their hearts lifted up who have betaken themselves off, with body and heart as well, to the marketplace outside? Or how shall they exclaim in awe mixed with gladness, *Sanctus, sanctus, sanctus, benedictus qui venit in nomine Domini?* Or again,

[7] *Hom. in II Cor.,* XVIII: *P.G. LXI,* 527, 529.

when the *Pater Noster* is said, who will there be to cry
in all humility and truth *Dimitte nobis,* etc., [Forgive
us our trespasses], and the rest ?" [8]

St. Paul wanted Christian prayers understood, as was
seen, so that the *Amen* could be answered (I Cor. xiv,
16). That oft-answered *Amen* was an inheritance
from Old Testament times, an inheritance that was
highly cherished. The *Didache,* written, it would
seem, some years before the death of St. John, the
Evangelist, gives us a Eucharistic prayer concluding
with its *Amen.* Our oldest Mass-descriptions, Justin's,
around 160, twice insists on this *Amen,* and since the
word would be unfamiliar to his readers, Justin is at
pains to explain it : "When he has concluded the prayers and the thanksgiving [he writes], all the people
who are present express their assent by saying *Amen.*
This word, *Amen,* means in the Hebrew language : So
be it ! And when the presiding official has celebrated
the Eucharist, and all the people have assented . . ." [9]
St. Jerome boasts that this *Amen* at the end of the
Mass-Canon fairly thundered across Rome : "Where
can the *Amen* be heard to resound as it resounds at
Rome, with a noise of thunder shaking the empty
temples of the idols?" [10] That particular *Amen,* as
said at Rome, and the responding to *Amen* in general,
also thundered through the entire patristic literature,
and, as we shall see, when the people's answering of
the *Amen* is testified to at the close of the Middle
Ages, in nearly every case the witness comes from
Rome. So, too, of the other short responses, *Deo
gratias, Et cum spiritu tuo* and the like.

[8] St. Cæsarius of Arles: cf. Migne, *P.L.* XXXIX, 2277: the English rendering is Father Thurston's.
[9] St. Justin, *Apology,* c. 65: cf. also c. 67: *P.G.;* XI, 427, 28; 429, 30.
[10] St. Jerome, *In Epist. ad Gal.,* II, Præf.: *P.L.* XXVI, 351.

Shall we consider the item of congregational singing in the early centuries? The Proconsul Pliny's letter to Trajan of 111 or 112 says that he had learned from apostate Christians that "the amount of their fault or error was this : That they had been accustomed to assemble on a fixed day before day-light and sing by turns a hymn to Christ as a god . . ." [11] The *Kyrie Eleison* would seem to owe its use by Christians to the fact that it was a popular refrain to be heard in the streets in pagan worship. As introduced into the Roman Mass by St. Gregory the Great, the *Kyrie* was led by the clergy and answered by the people, but later on the *schola* of trained singers took the lead, while the congregation continued the responding. St. Gregory says of its popularity in his day that it was crowding other prayers out of the weekday Masses. "In everyday Masses we omit certain parts which are wont to be said, saying only *Kyrie eleison* and *Christe eleison* in order that we may be engaged a little longer [than usual] in these deprecatory prayers." [12]

Novena devotions and a hundred other forms of worship demonstrate the popularity of litany-prayer with a simple, recurrent response (said), or refrain (sung) : the *Kyrie* of the Mass is one of the original models for this type of worship among Christians. It is, too, along with the *Gloria,* one of the parts which the modern papacy has decreed that the people "be made once more to sing." [13]

11 Pliny to Trajan, c. 7: cf. C. Kirch *Enchiridion Fontium Historiae Ecclesiasticae Antiquae* (Friburgi: Herder, 1910), 19.
12 St. Gregory Great, Epist. IX, 12: Migne, *P.L.* LXXVII, 956.
13 Pope Pius X, Letter of Cardinal Vicar, February 2, 1912: "Inviting the people to cooperate in this matter by taking a more active part in sacred functions by singing the *Kyrie,* the *Gloria,* etc., at High Mass . . .": *Catholic Church Music* (London: Burns, Oates and Washbourne, Ltd.), 1933, 27.

The introduction of the *Sanctus* into the Mass is recorded by saying that Pope Xystus I "decreed that [even] within the Action the priest should commence and the people take up the song, *Sanctus, Sanctus, Sanctus, Dominus Deus Sabbaoth.*" [14]   In the Carolingian age, when the vernacular was differentiating itself more and more from the Latin of the altar, Charles the Great ordered: "That the *Gloria Patri* [at the Introit, etc.] be sung with all honor by all present, and that the priest, together with the angels and the common voice of the people of God, should sing: '*Sanctus, Sanctus, Sanctus . . .*'" [15]   The Agnus Dei was introduced into the Mass of Rome by Pope Sergius I (687-701), in whose official biographical sketch is recorded: "It was his decree that at the moment of the breaking of the Body of the Lord, 'Lamb of God, who takest away the sins of the world, have mercy on us,' be sung by clergy and the people." [16]   The Creed first became part of the Mass in the West in Spain by decree of the Third Council of Toledo (589): "That in all churches of Spain or Galicia, after the manner of the Eastern churches, the rule of faith of the Council of Constantinople . . . be recited, so that, before the *Our Father* it be sung in a clear tone by the people." [17]   In 810 Charlemagne sent an embassy to Rome to petition that the Creed be sung in the Mass in his realms. [18]   It probably owes its position in *our* Mass, right after the Gospel, to the fact that it was customary even then to have Peoples' Prayers after the Gospel. [19]

---

[14] *Liber Pontificalis*, edit. Duchesne I, 128.
[15] *MGH Capitularia*, I, 59.
[16] *Liber Pontificalis*, edit. Duchesne I, 376.
[17] J. Brinktrine, *Die Heilige Messe in Ihrem Werden und Wesen* (Paderborn: Schöningh, 1931), 96, 97.
[18] Brinktrine, 97.
[19] *Ibid.*, 97.

This matter of popular participation by song became, of course, increasingly difficult the wider grew the breach between Latin and the language of the commonfolk. It became a moral impossibility, as will be shown at greater length in another place, when the simple chants were replaced by intricate musical compositions.

Shall we say a word of that striking mode of participation in the sacrifice, by which individual worshippers brought their gift-offerings to the altar? St. Hippolytus of Rome, about 225, refers to this usage in his *Apostolic Tradition* when speaking of baptismal candidates, and his is the earliest such reference known to me. Hippolytus says that the neophytes coming to Baptism are to bring with them "no other vessels than the one each shall bring for the Eucharist: for it is right for him who is worthy to bring his oblation then." [20] What might seem uncertain in this casual reference is surely clear enough in the writing of St. Cyprian, about 250, where he says with an acerbity very rare in his pages: "You are wealthy and rich, and imagine that you celebrate the Lord's Supper though you give no thought to the gift-offering. You come to the Lord's Supper without a sacrifice, and receive [at Communion] a portion of the sacrifice which the poor offer." [21] St. Augustine says in his simple eloquent praise of St. Monica: "She let no day pass without putting her sacrifice upon the altar." [22] How far from our modern conditions seems the background of this decree of a national council in Gaul (585): "Since

[20] St. Hippolytus, *Apostolic Tradition*, 20: cf. R. Connolly, "The So-Called Egyptian Church Order and Derived Documents," *Texts and Studies*, VIII, 4 (Cambridge, 1916), 183.
[21] St. Cyprian, *De Opere et Eleemosynis*, c. 15: *P.L.* IV, 612-13.
[22] St. Augustine, *Confess.* v, 9: *P.L.* XXXII, 714.

we have assembled we have learned from the report of
brethren that some Christians in some places have de-
viated from the divine command — in not offering a
host at the sacred altar.   Wherefore we decree that on
every Sunday an offering be made at the altar by all,
men and women, that by those oblations they may obtain remission of their sins and may deserve to be shar-
ers with Abel and the rest of just offerers." [23]

Nothing has been said bearing directly on the tradition of the people making the short responses with the
server at low Masses.   Here we are seriously handi-
capped by the fragmentary state of our information
about the history of low Mass as such.   It is not
known, as was said, when low Mass began to be used,
nor is it known just how it was celebrated.   This
much is certain : no shred of evidence has come to my
knowledge indicating that the people's responding was
restricted by any prescription high or low.   The ru-
brication of the early Mass-books, extremely sparse at
best, makes no differentiation between low Mass and
high Mass, and it is not possible to affirm with certainty that such rubrics as, *respondet populus, respondet plebs, respondent omnes,* etc., were an accurate reflex of what happened at low Mass.   In the
period, 600-900, there is abundant manuscript evidence that all responded at high Mass : the rubric
respondet populus of a famous Gregorian Sacramen-
tary was so well-known that it is found in a later recen-
sion as RP.[24]   It would dispel every possibility of

[23] Council of Macon: *Mansi*, IX, 951: translation quoted is that of
Herbert Thurston.
[24] Reference is made here to MSS, *Padua D* 47 and *St. Gall* 348, each of
which has been edited in the series, *Liturgiegeschichtliche Quellen*, 11-12
(Münster, 1927) and 1-2 (Münster, 1917).   The pertinent data are indicated in G. Nickl, *Der Anteil des Volkes an der Messliturgie im Franken-
reiche* (Innsbruck: Rauch, 1930), 9, 10.

doubt if the rubric had added "even at low Mass," but such it did not do.

Shortly before he became pope as Innocent III, Cardinal Lotario de'Conte published a famous work, *De Sacrificio Missae.* The basis of his commentary is a solemn pontifical Mass, but Innocent did not limit his exposition to that type of Mass. The officiant, he says, "confesses his sins with those standing around" (*cum astantibus*: c. 13); at the end of the Collects "the people respond by assenting *Amen*" (c. 26); the *Orate Fratres* "is most fittingly answered by many" (*respondeatur a pluribus*, c. 25), and so forth.[25]

Two generations or so after Innocent's book made its triumphant journey through Christendom, the writings of St. Thomas of Aquino were beginning a similar and greater progress. Well, the treatment of the Eucharist, in the Third Part of the *Summa*, is the Angelic Doctor at his very best, just before a premature death struck the pen from his fingers. Where the offering of Mass is being dealt with, it is high Mass that is doubtless actually mirrored, but after the high Mass, Thomas' words apply with far greater force to Dialog Mass than to a "silent" low Mass. He teaches:

"As was said above, those things are mentioned in this Sacrament which belong to the entire Church; and consequently some things which refer to the people are sung by the choir, and some of these words are all sung by the choir, as though inspiring the entire people with them; and there are other words which the priest begins and the people take up, the priest then acting as in the person of God; . . . and therefore the priest intones the *Creed* and the *Gloria in excelsis Deo.*

[25] Innocent III, *De Sacrificio Missae: P.L.* 217, 763 *sqq.*

"Other words are uttered by the ministers, such as
the doctrine of the Old and New Testament, as a sign
that this doctrine was announced to the peoples
through ministers sent by God.   And there are other
words which the priest alone recites, namely such as
belong to his personal office, that he may offer up gifts
and prayers for the people (Heb. v. 1).   Some of these,
however, he says aloud, namely, such as are common
to priest and people alike, such as the common prayers ;
other words, however, belong to the priest alone, such
as the oblation and the consecration ; consequently,
the prayers that are said in connection with these have
to be said by the priest in secret.   Nevertheless, in
both he calls the people to attention by saying : *The
Lord be with you,* and he waits for them to assent by
saying *Amen.*   And therefore, before the secret prayers
he says aloud, *The Lord be with you,* and he concludes, *Forever and forever.*" [26]

The same St. Thomas answered the objection that
Mass, being essentially social and communal, ought
never be said in private or by a priest alone, by saying
that the server takes the place of the entire Catholic
people, on whose behalf he answers in the plural. The
passage follows:

"Several persons ought to be present at the solemn
celebration of the Mass. . .   Nevertheless, in private
Masses it suffices to have one server, who takes the
place of the whole Catholic Church, on whose behalf
he makes answer in the plural to the priest." [27]

If Thomas had been asked about the propriety of
the whole people making the responses with the server,
or reciting at low Mass what they sang at high Mass, in

[26] St. Thomas, *The Summa Theologica of St. Thomas Aquinas* (London: Burns, Oates and Washbourne, 1923), XVII, 452, 53.
[27] St. Thomas, *loc. cit.,* 462.

the light of what he taught about the celebration of
the Mass, what would his reply have been?

One does not often appeal to the Council of Basle
for an expression of the true mind of the Church, yet
Hefele and others admit that, prior to the Bull,
September, 1437, ordering the Council transferred to
Ferrara, Basle was a true, oecumenical Council. In
its orthodox, if not necessarily oecumenical, period,
the Council passed a decree dealing for the most part
with abuses in the celebration of the Divine Office.
A few abuses relating to high Mass were included, and
then followed these provisions:

"And [the abuses] of low Mass being said without a
server, or where, besides the secret prayers, low Mass
is said in such a low tone that it cannot be heard by
those attending, we abolish these abuses, and have decreed that whoever be found guilty in these matters be
condignly punished by his superior."[28]

True, the Council did not say that the bystanders
were *to answer* to what they heard, but that this was
the mind of the Church at Rome is put beyond all
doubt, it seems to me, by the facts relative to the *Ordo
Missae* of John Burckard. Burckard, after years of
service as Papal Master of Ceremonies, published in
1502 a revision of his *Ordo Missae*.[29] Alexander VI,
the reigning pope, states in an accompanying letter,
that he had Cardinal Bernardin de Carvajal carefully
revise Burckard's work. Once published, Burckard's
Ordo Missae was reprinted in missals and elsewhere
time after time. Legg, Burckard's modern editor, has
listed twenty-eight known editions of the work falling
between 1502 and 1572, five at Rome, nineteen at

[28] Council of Basle, June 9, 1435: cf. *Mansi*, XXIX, 107.
[29] J. Burckard: cf. J. W. Legg, *Tracts on the Mass* (London: Bradshaw
Society, 1904); Introduction, xxv-xxviii; Text, 121-178.

Venice, two as far east as Cracow, one as far west as Lisbon, one as far north as Lyons. A Venetian edition of 1523 claims on its title page the approbation of Pope Leo X. And, when St. Pius V, in response to the request of the Council of Trent, published the "standardized" *Missale Romanum* in 1570, its rubrical section, *Ritus Servandus,* is based on Burckard's *Ordo Missae* : Here are Burckard's directions for the responses made by others than the server, and side by side with them the corresponding passages of our modern Mass-books.

BURCKARD'S *Ordo Missae* (1502)	*Missale Romanum* (1570 to today)
After the verse, *Iudica* : "The server and those present say each of the other or secondary verses, and respond to the other things as indicated below." (Legg, 135)	After the verse, *Iudica* : "The priest continues with the server or servers alternately . . ." (*Ritus Servandus,* III, 6)
After the *Confiteor* : "The Supreme Pontiff, a cardinal, a legate, a patriarch, an archbishop, or bishop, and the server and those present, kneeling say . . ." (Legg, 136)	After the *Confiteor* : "When the server and those present even in case the Supreme Pontiff be there, answer the *Confiteor* . . ." "The *Confiteor* being said by the bystanders . . ." (*Ritus Servandus,* III, 9, 10)
After the *Kyrie* : "If the server or those present do not make the responses, the celebrant himself says the whole." (Legg, 139)	After the *Kyrie* : "If the server or those present do not make the responses, the celebrant himself says nine times." (*Ritus Servandus* IV, 2)

Burckard's *Ordo Missae* (1502)	*Missale Romanum* (1570 to today)
At the *Orate Fratres*: "The server and those present, kneeling, with heads uncovered, respond." (Legg, 152)	At the *Orate Fratres*: "And the response, *Suscipiat* . . . being made by the server or bystanders . . ." (*Ritus Servandus*, VII, 7) "The server, or those standing by, respond, else the priest himself says . . ." (*Ordo Missae, ad loc.*)

Thus, most of Burckard's directions for congregational responding have carried right over into our modern Mass-books.

If Burckard had had a publisher at Bruges, or Louvain, or Cologne, even Paris, or even London, a Spanish cardinal's secretary would not have remarked in 1518, I am inclined to think, that the priests of the Low Countries did not permit any to make the low Mass responses, save only the server. But if the priests of Flanders were then to some extent singular in restricting the laity's responses in this way, the priests of modern Flanders have led the vanguard towards the universal restoration of this mode of active lay participation in the low Mass of the West.

CHAPTER III

RISE AND SPREAD OF DIALOG MASS[1]

In the sixteenth century the custom still survived, at Rome and elsewhere, that the congregation made the Mass-responses with the server. When the custom disappeared is not known. When Pope Benedict XIV published in full pontificate, so to speak, his *De Sacrosancto Sacrificio Missae* in 1748, he spoke of the practice as no longer obtaining: "Formerly the people in attendance were accustomed to respond to the celebrant, as Visconti proves with irrefragable arguments in his book. . ."[2] Whether the old usage just died of itself, or was terminated by some positive action, we do not know. If the latter should prove to have been the case the reason, doubtless, would be a reaction against the Jansenists' efforts to force similar practices on the Church. This connection with Jansenism, in Tuscany itself, in the very shadow of the Vatican, well merits momentary attention. But, to see the connection, one must first glance back to the Council of Trent.

Not a few of these abuses which gave Luther reason

[1] The data in this chapter on the early history of the Dialog Mass are derived chiefly from G. Lefebvre's "La Question de la Messe Dialoguée," *La Participation Active des Fidèles au Culte*, (Louvain: Mont-César, 1934), 143-196. This study is cited as *Lefebvre*.

[2] Benedict XIV, *De Sacrosancto Sacrificio Missae* (Italian, then Latin, Rome, 1748), lib. I, cap. xi, n.1: Dicimus quondam populum adstantem sacerdoti celebranti respondere consuevisse, quod invictis probat argumentis Vicecomes *de antiquis Missae ritibus* 1. I, c. 14. In the modern edition of Benedict's work, J. Schneider (Moguntiae: Kircheim, 1879), this passage is on page 71. The work cited by Benedict is J. Visconti (Vicecomes), *Observationes ecclesiasticae de antiquis missae ritibus* (Mediolani, 1620).

for solemnly appealing to this Council (which, however, he did not attend), were related to public worship, were associated with the fact that for ages the layman was being deprived by force of circumstances of an active and intelligent part in divine worship. All this, it was then hoped, would be remedied by this great Council.

Indeed Trent planned a complete program of reform of Catholic public worship. The Council's solicitude was most in evidence in all that referred to holy Mass, because, as the Fathers said, "of all holy things this Sacrifice is the most holy." In resisting the Protestant demands, the Council deemed it "inadvisable that Mass should be celebrated everywhere in the vulgar tongue." Yet on all having the care of souls it laid the obligation, "lest the little ones ask for bread and there be none to break unto them, to explain frequently during the celebration of the Mass, especially on Sundays and festival days . . . some mystery of this most holy Sacrifice."

If Trent similarly rejected the Reformers' petition that the entire Mass be said aloud, it did reaffirm "that some things in the Mass be pronounced in a low tone and others in a loud voice." In opposition to the heretical position, Masses at which the priest alone communicated were held to be valid Masses, yet in crystal-clear language it affirmed the desirability of having all worshippers at Mass communicate: "The Holy Council wishes indeed that at each Mass the faithful who are present should communicate, not only in spiritual desire, but also by the sacramental partaking of the Eucharist, that thereby they may derive from this most holy Sacrifice a more abundant fruit." The texts of the Missal and the Breviary were deemed to need correction, mostly in the nature of excision, and this work, begun at the Council, was then turned over to the Holy See for completion. In a hundred minor ways the Council showed its zeal that anything savoring in the least degree of unworthiness be kept from the public worship of the Church.

The thorny problem of having only proper music in the churches was given much more serious consideration than might be judged from the brevity of this statement: "They [local Ordinaries] shall also banish from the churches those types of music in which, whether by the organ or in the singing, there is mixed up anything unbecoming, . . . so that the house of God may be truly a house of prayer." Indeed, many a bishop at the Council may have had painful experience of the force of that saying, that more people were sung into Protestantism than argued into it. As early as 1523, in his *Form for Mass and Communion,* Luther had stressed the desirability of vernacular singing: "I would wish among *us* to have as much as possible in the vernacular what the people sing at Mass." Within the year Luther had contributed no less than twenty of his own compositions to this musical side of his revolt, and after *Eine feste Burg* had won its sensational reputation, religious rebels in non-German lands began to sweep people into their conventicles by affording them the chance to sing at divine service. Small wonder that the Fathers of Trent, with all this before their very eyes, wished to purge away the corruption that had overlaid the Church's once so popular plainsong. This once restored to the *people,* they would be saved the sad choice of active participation in unorthodox worship, or mute and silent worship in the Church of Rome.

Vigorously the Holy See set its hand to the carrying through of this worship-reform. In Italy and in the reconquered parts of the Germanies, the restoration of Holy Communion was making the most gratifying progress. Naturally the new liturgical texts were a primary concern : these began to appear within five years after the Council's close, the Breviary in 1568, the Missal in 1570, the Pontifical in 1596, and the Ritual in 1614.

But as early as Oct. 1, 1567, Rome had seen itself forced to condemn some doctrinal errors of Michael du Bay, which meant that the Church was already engaged in a second gigantic struggle, this one destined to last two full centuries, with a movement we call Jansenism, and which gives in a word the reason why the long-planned reforms of worship suffered yet another long delay.

That movements even the most excellent from every point of view have their appointed day, and must await their time, would seem to be a moral of this liturgical revival. At least there could be no sound liturgical revival while Jansenism held the field. Scarcely was that ultra-rigorist movement born in the Low Countries, when it found such shelter in influential quarters that it could maintain itself, despite repeated condemnations, for two hundred years. It infected practically all of Christendom that had not gone into Protestantism. The Bourbon kings of France, its chief defenders, were linked in such close ties of blood and policy with the royal houses of Spain and Portugal, the dependent duchies of Italy, and the imperial house of Austria, that this combination of princes, who had the appointment to bishoprics in their hands, made all effective reform from the side of Rome impossible.

What made Jansenism one of the worst threats and menaces the Church has ever faced was its persistent refusal to acknowledge itself condemned — or cut off. When Benedict XIV, who was mentioned above, was elected pope in 1740, almost two centuries had elapsed since Baianism had been condemned, one full century since *Augustinus* and Arnauld's book against frequent Communion, full sixty years since the adoption of the infamous Gallican Articles, thirty years since the Bull, *Unigenitus,* was to have put a stop once and for all to the movement, and, after wrestling his entire pontificate with it, Benedict knew at the end that the movement was firmly entrenched and defiant.[3]

In its final and most daring phases Jansenism aimed at, and to some extent realized, a most sweeping "liturgical reform," besides which the measures planned at Trent were insignificant indeed. In France, at the start, the breviary, missal, ritual and other manuals of the Roman Rite were abandoned, and fresh rites were composed, in Latin to be sure, but in the spirit of antipapal and heretical bias. Arnauld pleaded for a full vernacular liturgy, and Rome countered with making it a matter of excommunication to publish the missal-prayers in the vernacular. Eighty dioceses of France had their local Jansenist-tinctured Latin service-books, but beyond that the matter did not go under Louis XIV or Louis XV.

In the Germanies Emperor Joseph II came forward with sheaves of regulation about the number of Masses to be permitted, the composition and arrangement of Masses, the use of the vernacular, the number of altars

---

[3] Benedict XIV and Jansenism, cf. L. Pastor, *Geschichte der Päpste* (Freiburg: Herder, 1931), XVI, 1, 161-208.

in the churches, the ordering of flowers and candles and so forth, which earned for him from Frederick the Great the sobriquet, "My Brother, the Sacristan." People laughed, but under the "Sacristan's" direction all manner of "reforms" were set on foot. Missals for altar-use in German were published in more than one city, and at Stuttgart, for instance (there were other cities, too), Mass for a time was celebrated in German.[4] That was in 1786.

Caesar in the sacristy was bad enough, and Rome could do nothing but protest. But in Italy, Caesar's brother and successor as emperor, Leopold, Duke of Tuscany, found a bishop pliant enough to put all this into synodal legislation. Bishop Ricci of Pistoia got the entire Jansenist program into the form in which it was hoped to foist it upon the Church in Italy. The date, again, is 1786, and it marks the high-water level of the anti-papal flood. In 1789 the fall of the Bastille brought many a hollow pretension crashing down with it: in 1790 Bishop Ricci's protecting shield, Leopold, left Italy to ascend the imperial throne; whereupon there was rioting in Tuscany, public burning of the priests' "Italian" missals and other indications of the popular instinct for what is right.[5] Rome was free to institute an official examination of the Pistoian legislature. The manifold strictures listed against Ricci's reforms were not published until 1794, by which date royalty and bishops alike in France had atoned in blood for their rebellious attitude against the Holy

[4] V. Thalhofer, *Handbuch der Katholischen Liturgik* (Freiburg: Herder, 1883), I, 113: in the subsequent recasting of this work by Msgr. Ludwig Eisenhofer, the materials here alluded to have been displaced.
[5] Mass in Italian: Pastor, *Geschichte der Päpste* (Freiburg: Herder, 1933), XVI, 3, 106: on riots, Pastor, Thalhofer, *et al.*

See. Among the provisions of Pistoia singled out for condemnation many refer to public worship, this one among them :

"66. The proposition, asserting that 'it would be [for the Catholic Church to act] contrary to the Apostolic practice and the counsels of God, unless easier methods were provided [in her public worship] to enable the people to unite their voices with the whole Church,' as understood of the [compulsory] introduction of the vernacular into liturgical prayer, — false, temerarious [unreasonably rash], destructive of the prescribed order for the celebration of the Mysteries, easily productive of many evils." [6]

That is why I feel sure that, if positive action were at that time taken to snuff out the flicker of congregational responding which the Middle Ages had handed on to modern times, it was the insistence of heretics and heretically-minded Catholics that supplied the incentive. And when Jansenism was at last swept out of the temple, the task of truly reforming Catholic worship was taken up afresh.

* * *

"Endeavor should be made as far as possible to restore Gregorian plainsong to the use of the people." This is the keystone of Pius X's reform structure, "in order that the faithful may once again take a more active part in ecclesiastical functions, as was the custom in olden times." [7] But is it only at a *high Mass* that, in Pius's words, "active participation in the

[6] Pistoian legislation: Denzinger-Bannwart, *Enchiridion Symbolorum* (Friburgi: Herder, 1932), No. 1566, 434.

[7] Words of Pius X, repeated in letter of his Cardinal Vicar, and quoted from *Catholic Church Music* (London: Burns, Oates and Washbourne, 1933), 5, 22, 23.

sacred mysteries is the primary and indispensable source
of the true Christian spirit?" Do not the rubrics of
the missal indicate in four places that the responses
may be said by the people? And, if singing the *Gloria,*
the *Credo,* the *Sanctus* and *Agnus Dei* together at high
Mass is so beneficial, would not reciting them together
at low Mass be some approximation of the religious
values of congregational song? So zealous priests began to think and to reason with the decrees of Pius X
in their hands.

"It was the Gregorian *Motu proprio* that was my
inspiration : I applied to low Mass of every day what
His Holiness says of the solemn or Sunday Mass." So
spoke a Belgian priest of Sommerain, in the diocese of
Namur, in giving an account of "The Assistance of
Children at Daily Mass" at a Eucharistic Congress at
Malines, 1909. "I used sheets of Bristol board, seventeen and one-half inches by fourteen [.44 x .35 cm.],"
this Father Piérard continued, "which I set up on a
lectern, presenting in a manner legible to thirty or
forty children, with the pauses indicated, all that my
group should say, on a given tone, in a loud voice, but
without 'elocution,' throughout the entire Mass, so as
to enable individual as well as group to fulfill the role
of active participant."[8] There were similar reports
from other sources at the International Eucharistic
Congresses of Montreal in 1910 and in 1911 at Madrid.
It is not without its own curious interest to note that
at this great Montreal assembly, Canon Campeau of
Ottawa, in advocating the use of acclamatory prayers
during Holy Hour exercises, drew out the thought
that people thus initiated would learn to follow the

[8] *Lefebvre,* 178-79.

Mass according to the ancient form of corporate worship among Christians.

In that summer of 1911, to revert again to Belgium, this manner of assisting at Mass was dealt with in a paper at the Liturgical Week at Mont-César, Louvain. "At low Masses," said the speaker, Dom de Meester, "the organic participation of the faithful is often almost nothing: one believes he has done everything in silently reading the principal parts of the Mass. . . Why could not the faithful there recite what they sing at high Mass, and what the server says? This has already been tried in various places, and the effect produced by this new mode of uniting the people present to the acts and prayers of the celebrant has surpassed all hopes. . . And as to the lawfulness of this method, we say that the Ordinaries have already given and will give their approbation [no doubt he meant locally] to these liturgical uses which refresh and arouse the devotion of their flocks to the Mass." [9] These words, particularly as seconded by the accounts appearing in print of the success attending priests' initial efforts, carried conviction a long way in Belgium.

As early as 1913, in the diocese of Bois-le-Duc, Holland, a diocesan liturgical commission took the position that, while the "new" mode of Mass-worship was quite licit in theory, still in practice it would have to be referred to the judgment of the Ordinary.[10]

The Flemish *Liturgish Tijdschrift* carried a series of articles in 1914 on "The Joint Answers of the People to the Prayers of the Priest," by Monsignor C. Callewaert, whose *Liturgicae Institutiones* are a semi-

9 *Lefebvre*, 179.
10 *Lefebvre*, 181.

nary classic.[11]   And in the world-encircling reverbera-
tions emanating from an assassin's weapon in Sarajevo
that summer, a thin, faint note might have been heard
gradually encompass the globe : it was the term, "Dialog Mass," then coined in Belgium and soon to be
used far and wide.[12]

Dialog Mass soon made its appearance in the Allied
camps in 1915, just a stone's throw from that locality,
where it was remarked in 1518 that the priests differed
from those of Rome, in that they did not allow any to
make the responses, save only the server.   In the matter of method the Dialog Mass made various trials, but
all in all guided itself along the simple and organic
lines traced by de Meester, "reciting what they sing at
high Mass and what the server says."   Thus, Catholics
in France, particularly in the north, in the Rhenish
and Bavarian sections of Germany, throughout Austria, and to a much less extent Catholics in Spain, England and Italy were in the course of the war becoming
familiar with Dialog Mass.   One after another the
dioceses of Holland set up Priests' Diocesan Liturgical
Associations (study and action clubs, we should name
them).

But from first to last the position of the Dialog Mass
was more favorable in Belgium than anywhere else.
This may be set down as one of the happiest by-prod-
ucts, so to speak, of the *entente cordiale* so long existing
between His Eminence Cardinal Mercier (†1926) and
Dom Columba Marmion, Abbot of Maredsous (†1923).
Marmion for years occupied the position of one of the
fountain-heads of the Catholic spirit in Belgium, and,

11 Monsignor Callewaert's articles, published originally in Flemish, were
later condensed and published in Latin, "De Liceitate Missae Dialogatae,"
in *Collationes Brugenses*, xxxii, 1932, 220-227.
12 *Lefebvre*, 181.

as was seen towards the end, he had providentially enriched the popular mind with the dogmatic and ascetic ideas latent in the communal piety of what was beginning to be called "the liturgical movement." Towards this movement Marmion had once defined his attitude and that of his Benedictine brethren in these words:

"If the sons of St. Benedict take such an active interest in the 'liturgical movement,' this is not only because, as religious, faithful to the mission of their order, they continue a tradition of fourteen centuries — it is still more so because, as most loving sons of holy Church, they endeavor with all their power to second the wishes of their holy Mother. Now, for some years, the Holy Spirit, who is the Soul of the Church, has urged her to revive the knowledge and the love of ritual prayer and sacred service in her children, to show them in the liturgy the 'primary and indispensable source of the true Christian spirit.' We, therefore, consider it a duty to enter into the views of the Vicar of Jesus Christ, and to place our feeble resources, material, moral and intellectual, at the disposition of Christians zealous for divine worship." [13]

Whether it was at Marmion's Abbey of Maredsous or not, that the heroic Archbishop of Malines, spiritual son, friend and associate of the Abbot, first became acquainted with the Dialog Mass, he was tremendously impressed by it. "The Dialog Mass," he wrote later on, "has edified me more than once in our colleges and in certain religious houses; nor have I concealed my sentiments of edification. But I have always desired that the practice be submitted to the approbation of the Congregation of Rites, or the Congregation of

[13] Columba Marmion: cf. *Orate Fratres*, I, 1 (November 28, 1926), 29.

the Sacraments. I spoke of it to Cardinal Ferrata, at that time Prefect of the Congregation of the Sacraments. His reply was : 'But why not? I see nothing in it at which to object ' " [14]

In 1920, when war-wracked Belgium was free to give its attention to the problems of peace, Cardinal Mercier presided over a National Council at Malines, with sessions in April and October. Besides the dogmatic, moral and sundry disciplinary decrees then enacted, there was a body of legislation dealing with pastoral and liturgical matters, of which one canon on communal participation in holy Mass is here given in translation.

"It is indeed regrettable [it began] that the faithful assisting at the most holy Sacrifice of the Mass for the most part conduct themselves, as if the Action were none of their concern. Hence we must set to work to make the Christian people really a [conscious] participant in the sacred Action. To accomplish this, one will have to proceed gradually, patiently and perseveringly."

Then dealing with high Mass the canon goes on to state :

"In the first place, let pastors strive that the solemn or high Mass have the chief place, and that its former esteem be restored to it, so that it will be considered, according to the sanction of antiquity, the true and solemn assembly of the entire parochial family. Let the faithful in attendance, as far as circumstances permit, have the liturgical texts of the Sunday Mass in hand, and the music of the common parts, in order that they be linked the more effectively (*efficacius*

14 *Lefebvre,* 186: The letter is dated March 25, 1921, but from what follows in our text on the Council of Malines in 1920, this letter must refer to a time a full year previously at least.

consocientur) with the Mysteries and feasts of holy
Church ; and let them be prepared for this sacred fel-
lowship by pious and solid explanations of the texts."

Low Mass is dealt with in the same spirit :

"To instill insensibly, as it were, in the minds of the
faithful that corporate and truly Christian spirit, and
to prepare the way for that active participation, which
the Holy See desires, one must praise the practice, at
least for educational institutions and religious houses,
whereby those present at Mass answer the responses in
unison with the acolytes.   (Canon 279)." [15]

This decree, praising the introduction of the Dialog
Mass, at least in educational institutions and religious
houses, was thereupon sent to Rome for approval.
Approval was delayed somewhat, no doubt in part
owing to the change in the pontificate with the death
of Pope Benedict XV and the election of Pope Pius
XI, and, it is quite possible, too, owing to the particular circumstances touching the Dialog Mass in
Italy just at that time.

Post-war Italian "reconstruction," we may remind
ourselves, was a particularly difficult and uneasy
period.   At the Peace Table, as it was called, Italians
as a people felt thwarted, humbled, disillusioned.
From September, 1919, to November, 1920, there was
one situation that can be described as little short of
voluntary anarchy : I refer to the fact that d'Annun-
zio's troops, in spite of governments and treaties, held
the city of Fiume against Yugoslavia.   In the hard
economic sphere there was a ruinous series of "seize-
the-factories" strikes, in the face of which the gov-
ernment was muddling and fumbling.   By secret
connivance, it would seem, arms, transportation and

---

[15] *Acta et Decreta* (Malines: Dessain, 1923), Canon 279.

protection were being furnished roving *squadristi* for violent attacks on "communists." Events were fast shaping themselves into a March on Rome. All in all, those were the days of bitter resentment, of restlessness verging on desperation.

Yet the Church continued to apply the healing of its offices to the wounds of the body politic. Two episodes will be instanced, one showing with evident satisfaction that the Dialog Mass was spreading in Italy, the other showing rather ominously what form it was taking in some places.

The Italian Saint Cecelia Society was to hold its twelfth annual convention in Turin, September, 1920. In preparation for this event, the organization's president addressed a circular to the entire Italian episcopate, which ended on this note

"Finally, the Association requests the Most Reverend Bishops, if it please them, to use their authority to recommend to religious communities of men and women, to educational institutions, to collaborate in a most uniform manner in promoting the active participation of all assisting at low Mass in alternately answering the priest in the responses and in reciting with him the *Gloria,* the *Credo,* the *Sanctus* and *Agnus Dei.* This custom has already been introduced in many places and has greatly increased devotion, attention and piety."

In reproducing in part this request in its pages, the semi-official *Osservatore Romano* adds that, as a matter of record, the Dialog Mass had already been introduced by many bishops in their dioceses.[16]

Yes, the Dialog Mass was spreading in Italy, but even in this letter there is a broad hint that this was

[16] *Lefebvre,* 184.

not being done uniformly. In fact, the *manner* in which the Dialog Mass was spreading, or shall we not rather say the *kind* of Dialog Mass that was making its presence conspicuous, was matter for serious concern on the score of propriety and reverence. At Imola, near Ravenna, at a Eucharistic Congress a speaker urged without reservations: "One cannot choose a better method of following the low Mass than to recite the sacred prayers at the same time as the priest." [17] It was not long before the loud recitation in Italian *of the entire Mass, the Canon and words of Consecration not excepted,* was spreading among religious houses and parish churches. It was not surprising that a query was sent to the Roman journal, *Ephemerides Liturgicae,* as to the supposed antiquity and actual propriety of such usage. The reply, of course, while praising the use of the Missal-prayers by the laity, said that the *loud recitation of the Canon* by the people was directly contrary to all ancient usage.[18] Beyond that statement the *Ephemerides,* as a private journal, had no authority to go. But bishops from far and near were applying to the Holy See for official guidance. This was being supplied them in customary curial channels until the number of requests seems to have prompted the insertion of a decree into the *Acta Apostolicae Sedis,* and its addition, later on, to the *Decreta Authentica* of the Sacred Congregation of Rites.[19]

It is to the careful examination of these decisions that we shall direct our attention in the next chapter.

[17] *Lefebvre,* 183; the passage is quoted in Italian in the *Ephemerides* as noted below.

[18] *Ephemerides Liturgicae,* xxxiv, 1922, 98, 99.

[19] *Acta Apostolicae Sedis,* XIV, 1922, 505: *Decreta Authentica Congregationis Sacrorum Rituum,* Appendix II, 39.

CHAPTER IV

THE HOLY SEE AND DIALOG MASS[1]

"The Dialog Mass must be condemned, as it is surely not free of the suspicion of heretical origin, and is clearly in opposition to many rubrics." At the close of the year 1921 an Italian prelate thus expressed himself in an ecclesiastical journal of Verona.[2] By the very vehemence of his language he was attacking at once on two fronts. Right before him there was confusion of conduct and thought as the result of a practice then springing up in Italy, by which the entire congregation recited aloud and in the vernacular the whole text of the Mass, Canon and words of consecration not excepted. Again, there was here and there and everywhere (it seemed) in Italy, France, Belgium, a strong case being built up in clerical journals for the Dialog Mass, in the ordinary sense of the term; the custom, namely, whereby people joined with the server in making the short responses, and joined with the priest in reciting *Gloria, Credo, Sanctus,* and *Agnus Dei.* And so, with devotion that was filial and zeal that was most orthodox, this Monsignor Pighi set

[1] This chapter is based, for the most part, on I. M. Hanssens, S.J., Professor of Liturgical Theology in the Gregorian University, "Vetera et Nova de Missa Dialogata," *Periodica,* XXV, 2 (April, 1936), 57*-89*. As before, I have also used Lefebvre, "La Question de la Messe Dialoguée," *La Participation Active des Fidèles au Culte* (Louvain: Mont-César, 1934), 152-196. These two works are cited below as *Hanssens* and *Lefebvre.*

[2] Msgr. G. B. Pighi, "Le Messa Dialogata," *Bollettino Ecclesiastico della Diocesi di Verona* (December, 1921-January, 1922), as quoted by J. Pauwels, S.J., in *Periodica,* XI (1923), 154-157.

out to slay this new thing that was penetrating Italy, from north to south, and his was not the only pen turned into rapier in this praiseworthy cause.[3]

To historically-minded prelates, such as Achille Ratti, for instance, who had become Cardinal-Archbishop of Milan that summer, would not this new and strange practice have seemed all but indistinguishable from the former abuse of vernacular Mass brought in by the Jansenists a century and a half before, and condemned by Pope Pius VI as "false, temerarious, destructive of the prescribed order for the celebration of the Mysteries, easily productive of many evils"?[4]

Thus, in 1922, Dialog Mass would seem by all appearances to have been headed straight for official banishment and condemnation. Yet both before and after Achille Ratti became Pope Pius XI, it was only the *inexpediency* of the Dialog Mass itself that was mentioned in the replies of the Sacred Congregation of Rites. Its introduction or non-introduction into a diocese was left to the decision of the local bishop.

Of course, the loud recitation of the Canon was condemned as an abuse, and its complete suppression decreed.

Within the space of three months the Congregation just mentioned handed down five replies that we know of, pertaining to this matter, and in the first of these it speaks of having made "like answers to similar petitions." Two of these five replies are duplicates, a third differs hardly at all: in the two other instances the text of the reply has not been made public.[5] In

---

[3] For a partial survey of this literature, cf. *Periodica* as just cited.

[4] H. Denzinger-C. Bannwart, *Enchiridion Symbolorum* (Friburgi: Herder, 1932), No. 1556, 434.

[5] February 18, 1921, to Bishop of Mantua: cf. *Ephemerides Liturgicae,* XXXV (1921), 33: also in *Hanssens;*

each reply of which the terms are known, the Sacred Congregation remits the decision as to the permissibility of the Dialog Mass to the local bishop, while deprecating it on that principle from St. Paul that "things that are in themselves licit, are not always expedient because of some difficulty." None of these responses was given official publication by the Holy See, and we need delay no longer over them.[6]

Within a few months of Pius XI's accession, August 4, 1922, the Sacred Congregation of Rites published the decree given here in English translation. It is now known as Decree 4375, S.C.R., and states:

"DOUBTS

CONCERNING THE BODY OF THE FAITHFUL ASSISTING AT MASS: MAY THEY ANSWER JOINTLY FOR THE SERVER, OR READ THE CANON IN A LOUD VOICE?

"The following doubts have been proposed to the Sacred Congregation for a timely answer, namely:
"I. May the congregation, assisting at the Sacrifice

February 25, to Bishop of Pesaro (near Rimini): *Eph. Lit.*, 313: also in *Hanssens;*
April 27, to Cardinal-Archbishop Mercier, Malines: was copy of the reply sent to Mantua, cf. supra;
May 7, to Abbot Ildephonse Schuster, St. Paul's, Rome: text not published: cf. *Lefebvre*, 186;
May 27, to Bishop of Metz, text not published: cf. *Lefebvre*, 186.
[6] In *Men at Work and Worship* (New York: Longmans, Green and Co., 1940), 143, I have indicated what a serious and misleading omission mars the publication of English versions of these documents in Bouscaren, *The Canon Law Digest*, II, (Milwaukee: The Bruce Publishing Co., 1937). Father Bouscaren has dropped out what are practically the most important words of the responses, *"Ad Rev. mum Ordinarium iuxta mentem"* and *".....ad mentem."* Father Hanssens adduces other examples from the decrees of the Congregation of Rites showing clearly that this formula remits the question to the local Bishop for decision by himself. One may consult, in this connection, Rev. William J. Lallou, "The Status of the 'Missa Recitata,'" *The American Ecclesiastical Review*, CIV, 5 (May, 1941), 455, or "The Dialog Mass." A. V. Gamble, C.PP.S., *Nuntius Aulae* (January, 1941), 2 *sqq.*

of the Mass, make the responses in unison, instead of the server?

"II. Is the practice to be approved, according to which the faithful assisting at Mass read aloud the Secrets, the Canon and the very words of Consecration, all of which except a very few words of the Canon should, according to the rubrics, be read secretly by the priest himself?

"REPLY: The Sacred Congregation of Rites, having heard the opinion of the Special Commission, and having considered everything carefully, has decided to reply:

"To the First Question: [The question is remitted] to the Most Reverend Ordinary [for decision] according to this norm. (*Ad Rev. mum Ordinarium iuxta mentem.*) The norm (*mens*) is: Things that are in themselves licet are not always expedient, owing to the difficulties which may easily arise, as in this case, especially on account of the disturbances which the priests who celebrate and the people who assist may experience, to the disadvantage of the sacred Action and of the rubrics. Hence, it is expedient to retain the common usage, as we have several times replied in similar cases.

"To the Second Question: [It is answered] in the negative; nor can the faithful who assist at Mass be permitted something that is forbidden by the rubrics to the priests celebrating, who say the words of the Canon secretly, for the sake of greater reverence towards the sacred Mysteries, and to enhance the veneration, modesty and devotion of the faithful: hence, the proposed practice is to be reprobated as an abuse, and if it has been introduced anywhere it is to be entirely removed.

"And it is thus replied, declared and decreed. August 4, 1922." [7]

This decree certainly put an end to the loud recitation of the Canon by the laity.   At first glance it might seem to have condemned Dialog Mass as well.   Yet the all-important difference between the response to the first question and to the second was thus indicated, happily I believe, by Reverend Joseph Pauwels, S.J., when the Decree appeared in *Periodica:*

"This Decree certainly does not favor Dialog Mass. Nor does it condemn it as something forbidden, but judges it inexpedient by reason of inconveniences that at the present time may easily arise from the practice.

"That the Sacred Congregation by no means wished to condemn Dialog Mass as illicit is clear in view of the different kind of reply to each of the two doubts proposed.   In the second query what is at stake is a practice, proposed perhaps by some extremists, but having nothing in common with Dialog Mass, as defended by the authors cited above.   In explicit terms it is severely condemned: *'In the negative;'* the practice mentioned *'is to be reprobated as an abuse,'* and, if anywhere introduced, *'is to be entirely removed.'* There is no such prohibition or condemnation in the reply to the first query, rather the contrary is not obscurely hinted at, *'things that are in themselves licet, are not always expedient.'* " [8]

Father Pauwels goes on to add editorially, and subsequent events have justified his conclusions a thousandfold, as we shall see: "Nothing, therefore, prevents the Bishop, if he judges that in certain circumstances, for example, in the chapel of a religious community, or

---

[7] Decree 4375: *Acta Apostolicae Sedis*, XIV (1922), 505: *Decreta Authentica Congregationis Sacrorum Rituum*, Appendix II, 39.

[8] J. Pauwels, S.J., cf. *Periodica*, XI (1923), 154-157.

seminary, or college, the practice of Dialog Mass be not the occasion of the inconveniences mentioned, from allowing it. . . , nor are we forbidden to hope that, little by little, under changed circumstances, the inconveniences will vanish, which will enable the Bishop to show himself lenient in granting the permission." [9]

As there is more to be said directly on the interpretation of this Decree, let us at this juncture run ahead of the narrative long enough to show how the Sacred Congregation itself has interpreted its own Decree.   Asked in 1935 by the Cardinal-Archbishop of Genoa for a fresh and comprehensive declaration of the Church's mind concerning Dialog Mass, the Congregation replied : "In accordance with Decree 4375 it is for the Ordinary to decide . . . According to the above standard, Your Eminence has the full authority to regulate this form of liturgical piety." [10]

Thirteen years intervened between these two replies of the Sacred Congregation, an interval in which the Dialog Mass, under episcopal sanction, was making an appearance in every quarter of the globe.   It must have been clear to the bishops and their chancery officials that they possessed, within the limitations of Decree 4375, "authority to regulate this form of liturgical piety."

Let us, for instance, take one particular case, the best documented one on record, to be true, and see how this bishop shaped his conduct in fullest obedience to the Holy See.   It is the case of Cardinal Mercier, Archbishop of Malines, primate of Belgium.   As

[9] J. Pauwels, S.J., cf. *Periodica*, XI (1923), 154-157.
[10] Decree of November 30, 1935: *Revista Diocesana* (Genoa, 1935).   The original Italian text is found in *Periodica* (XXV, 1936), 43, the Latin version in *Hanssens*, 61*-62*.

was pointed out previously, he had had an oral sanction from the Cardinal Prefect of the Congregation of
the Sacraments for the introduction of Dialog Mass.
He later asked for written sanction of the Congregation of Rites.   Under date of April 27, 1921, the Congregation sent him the response: "The question is
returned to yourself for decision according to this
norm : things that are in themselves licit are not always
expedient because of some difficulty, for example, if
such a practice would confuse one or several priests
who are celebrating . . ."[11] From which Cardinal
Mercier would conclude that, providing the difficulties
were obviated, he was free to permit and regulate
Dialog Mass. Three months later he received the
official promulgation of Decree 4375, wherein, as before, the final decision is left to the Bishop. True,
grounds for inexpediency are somewhat wider in this
Decree, but there was nothing to shake the Archbishop's confidence that, if episcopal zeal and guidance
overcame the difficulties, the inexpediency of Dialog
Mass would have ceased. Should the difficulties prove
insurmountable, then it would be well to retain the
common usage of "silent" Mass.

That conclusion on the part of the Cardinal-Archbishop did not long lack highest Vatican support, for
on November 16, 1922, the Sacred Congregation of
the Council gave formal approbation to this canon of
the Council of Malines two years before:

"To instill insensibly, as it were, into the minds of
the faithful that corporate and truly Christian spirit,
and to prepare the way for that active participation,
which the Holy See desires, one must praise the prac-

tice, at least for educational institutions and religious houses, whereby those present at Mass answer the responses in unison with the acolytes." [12]

So Cardinal Mercier proceeded to promulgate this decree, March 25, 1923. Parenthetically, it might be added for completeness' sake, that the possible disturbance to priests celebrating at side altars was precluded by ruling that there should be no such Masses during the people's Dialog Mass.

Shortly before the promulgation of this Roman-approved Belgian legislation, Cardinal Schulte, Archbishop of Cologne, promulgated a decree of one of his synods, which, without mentioning Dialog Mass in just so many words, did in fact give great impetus to the spread of the practice in Germany. Cardinal Schulte's decree declared itself inspired by the mind of Pius X:

"Pursuant to the admonition of Pope Pius X, 'not merely to pray during Mass but to pray the Mass,' those entrusted with the care of souls . . . will do their best to insure the closest possible participation of the faithful in the prayers of the Mass as uttered by the priest at the altar." [13]

Bishops in general terms, and in very specific terms, as will be set out in another connection, were using

[12] *Acta et Decreta* . . . (Malines: Dessain, 1923).

[13] Cologne Archdiocesan decree quoted from official publication (Köln: Bachem, 1922), 45, by Joseph Kramp, *Die Opferanschauungen der römischen Messliturgie* (Regensburg: Kösel-Pustet, 1924), 37: the English version of Kramp is *Eucharistia* (St. Paul: Lohmann, 1926), 158. This may be a suitable place to advert in passing to that controversy in the press some years ago as to whether Pope Pius X actually said the words attributed to him in this decree. *Orate Fratres*, IX, 526, closed the dispute in its pages with a frank *non liquet:* "It does not make much difference whether it can or cannot be proved that the saintly Pope actually said these words; but this phrase does in reality sum up perfectly his convictions as expressed on more than one occasion." The similar saying, "Do not sing at Mass, sing the Mass," it was brought out in this controversy, is demonstrably an authentic statement of Pius X.

the authority that Rome said they possessed to permit and watch over the Dialog Mass in their several jurisdictions.   The present survey limits itself to Italy.

Did Pope Pius XI use the eminence of his high position to endorse Dialog Mass by personal example? In his apostolic constitution "On Divine Worship" (*Divini cultus*) he did say: "It is most important that when the faithful assist . . . they should not be merely detached and silent spectators but . . . they should sing alternately with the clergy and choir, as it is prescribed." [14]   Save by inference there is no application of this principle to low Mass.   It has been reported more than once that Pius XI himself led the celebration of Dialog Mass.   The first such celebration was at the men's nocturnal adoration exercises in St. Peter's Basilica in the night of May 26-27, 1922, on the occasion of the International Eucharistic Congress in Rome.   Father (later Bishop) d'Herbigny, in an eyewitness' stirring description of the memorable event, says in part:

"Of a sudden, led by the priests, the multitude of the faithful recite with the Holy Father the *Gloria, Credo, Sanctus, Pater* and *Confiteor*.   What a spectacle before man and God, this low Mass of the Pope celebrated when the night was at quiet peace, the contrite adoration of these men, who though tired from a hot and fatiguing day were praying still, standing or kneeling on the floor for almost four hours. . . The endless distribution of the Bread of Life by the Pope himself, and by Bishops of every nation, race and color, the stillness of the enormous basilica tempered to the subdued pitch of a convent chapel . . . the prayerful absorption and unostentatious simplicity of

[14] Pius XI, *Divini Cultus: Acta Apostolicae Sedis*, XXI (1929), 39, 40.

that continuous effort of love toward God, this Eucharistic Tryst of Christendom at the tomb of the sainted Peter, all of this together, was it not a spectacle surpassing in grandeur the most pretentious manifestations of the ages that have marched before us?" [15]

Again it was reported at a Mass for French pilgrims during the jubilee year that the entire group responded throughout the Mass, and afterwards received the Pontiff's congratulations on the manner in which they had carried off their part of the joint celebration.[16] That pilgrims were not the only ones among Pius XI's subjects that enjoyed Dialog Mass at Rome is illustrated by the fact that His Excellency our Most Reverend Papal Delegate, Amleto G. Cicognani, then chaplain to university students in the Holy City, regularly celebrated Dialog Mass with them. Even yet it is a matter of gratification that "those young people, well instructed and prepared, did excellently." [17] Doubtless the wistful remembrance of his former Dialog Masses in Rome prompted the same Apostolic Delegate to act as he did on the occasion of the Catholic Charities Convention, Cincinnati, 1934, thus described in a lively manner by Bishop J. H. Schlarman:

"A few weeks ago the National Convention of Catholic Charities was held in Cincinnati. His Excellency, the Apostolic Delegate, sang the high Mass. The sermon was eloquent. How much of the sermon those who heard it remember today, I do not know. But

[15] M. d'Herbigny, "Le Congrès Eucharistique de Rome," *Études*, 171 (June, 1922), 709-711: I am indebted to Rev. D. A. Schmal, S.J., for this quotation. I have also heard Rev. Patrick Cummins, O.S.B., of Conception Abbey, who was present on that occasion, give a stirring account of the incident.

[16] Cf. *Orate Fratres,* IV, 1 (December 1, 1929), 41, quoting *Caldey Notes* (October, 1927).

[17] This item was given the author in a letter under date of February 25, 1941, and is quoted here with explicit authorization.

A. G. Cicognani
Apostolic Delegate to United States
Who in Rome regularly celebrated Dialog Mass

there was one thing far more powerful than the most eloquent sermon, and no one present will ever forget it. After the pontifical Mass, His Excellency, Archbishop McNicholas, ascended the pulpit and announced that the personal representative of the Holy Father, the Apostolic Delegate, would grant a plenary indulgence in the name of the Holy Father. Then came the startling announcement: Archbishop McNicholas said that it was the special and personal request of the Delegate — he repeated the statement — that the whole congregation recite the *Confiteor*. At last the people had a chance to *do something,* to make themselves heard, to take part in the service! Archbishop McNicholas led the *Confiteor*. The response on the part of the people was a tremendous outburst of pent-up feeling. They wanted to *do something*. They had waited two hours for this opportunity. That *Confiteor,* led by Archbishop McNicholas, and repeated by the whole congregation, will never be forgotten by any one who was present." [18]

"Shepherd the flock of God that is with you . . . becoming an example to the flock," Peter had written to his hierarchial helpers (I, v, 3). It is always the Bishop's highest praise that he shepherds the local flock after the mind and spirit of Peter's reigning successor. Well, in the matter here reviewed, the attitude of the Holy See to the Dialog Mass, Cardinal Schuster, successor to Pius XI in Milan, and their Excellencies of Bergamo, Brescia, Como, Crema, Cremona, Lodi, Mantua and Pavia, in a Joint Pastoral of 1927, thus spoke of Dialog Mass:

"To induct the young into the liturgical assistance

[18] J. H. Schlarman, "Minimum Liturgical Program," *Catholic Mind,* XXXIII, 6 (March 22, 1935), 118.

at holy Mass, we recommend, particularly in institutions and oratories, at the Children's Mass, the practice known as Dialog Mass, but avoiding the excess of having recited in loud tones the secret prayers or sacramental formulæ reserved exclusively to the priest." [19]

True, only children were envisaged as beneficiaries of the episcopal recommendation, but the grown-ups and the parish churches are alike the objects of this resolution adopted at the Liturgical Week held in Bergamo, April, 1931 :

"A means most useful in fostering the active participation of the faithful is to favor the use of the Dialog Mass in educational institutions, and even in parishes where the clergy are more numerous, and this within the limits and according to the forms approved by the Church." [20]

In mid-July, 1932, Cardinal Minoretti, Archbishop of Genoa, and his seven suffragans met in annual conference, at the conclusion of which this recommendation was made public : "One of the means for holding the attention of those at Mass on the alert consists in having the entire congregation, in lieu of the server or along with the server, answer those parts which the acolyte is accustomed to say." [21] What must have been the surprise of these bishops of Liguria, to say nothing of the other ecclesiastics in Italy, to hear a few weeks later of a violent attack on the very idea of Dialog Mass, as being something "simply, clearly and precisely condemned" by the Holy See in Decree 4375 ? "One must obey the Holy See, the Pope, always and unconditionally, even at the cost of one's own life,"

19 *Lefebvre*, 193.
20 *Lefebvre*, 193.
21 *Lefebvre*, 194.

argued the writer in fine fervor.[22]   This singular
challenge and contention provoked a literary war from
one end of Italy to the other, until, a year later, the
original writer publicly acknowledged that Decree
4375 gave the local bishop full authority to sanction
Dialog Mass if he saw fit.[23]

Divisions there must be that the truth appear in
fuller light.   It is doubtless owing to the world-wide
ramifications of the dispute just referred to that Cardinal Minoretti made formal appeal for a fresh response
from the Holy See.   It was from this reply that a few
words were cited in a previous paragraph : the entire
document is now presented.

"ROME, *Nov.* 30, 1935.

"Most Reverend Eminence :

"To the doubts which Your Eminence has proposed,
namely :

"I.   In Seminaries, religious houses, and in some
parishes a custom has become established whereby the
people, together with the server, make the responses
in low (*privatis*) Masses, provided that no confusion is
occasioned.   It is asked whether this practice may be
sustained, and even propagated.

"II.   In some places, at low (*privatis*) Masses, the
people recite aloud and in unison with the priest, the
Gloria, Credo, Sanctus, Benedictus and *Agnus Dei.*
The promoters of this practice give this reason : low
Mass is an abbreviated sung Mass.   Now in sung Mass
the people sing the *Gloria, Credo, Sanctus, Benedictus*
and *Agnus Dei.*   It is asked whether the practice and
the reason alleged for it can be sustained.

"This Sacred Congregation, having heard also the

---

[22] The attack appeared in *Messaggero del Sacro Cuore*, August and September, 1932.

[23] Cf. *Palestra del Clero* (July, 1933), cf. *Lefebvre*, 192.

opinion of the Liturgical Commission, replies that in accordance with Decree 4375 it is for the Ordinary to decide whether, in individual cases, in view of all the circumstances, namely, the place, the people, the number of Masses which are being said at the same time, the proposed practice, though in itself praiseworthy, in fact causes disturbance rather than furthers devotion. This can easily happen in the case of the practice mentioned in the second question, even without passing judgment on the reason alleged, namely, that the low Mass is an abbreviated sung Mass.

"According to the above standard, Your Eminence has the full right to regulate this form of liturgical piety according to your prudent discretion.

"Kissing the sacred purple. . ."[24]

Reverend I. J. Hanssens, S.J., Professor of Liturgical Theology at the Pontifical Gregorian University, seized the opportunity of the appearance of this new rescript to survey once more the entire question of the Dialog Mass in *Periodica,* thus affording us what is perhaps our best study on the subject.[25] From that magisterial essay come most of the data in these pages. Comparing the new rescript with the former ones, Father Hanssens points out, discloses that on the part of the Holy See the same guiding principle has been present from first to last, whereas on the part of the questioners the intervening years had brought no little progress and clarification of thought. In place of the former temerity and confusion as to the organic nature of active lay participation in low Mass, there has been substituted little by little greater understanding and prudence. Hence there is a correspondingly greater

[24] Italian version, *Periodica,* XXV (1936), 43; Latin version *Hanssens,* 61*-62*.

[25] Cf. Footnote 1, above.

benevolence towards Dialog Mass in the language of the rescript.[26] The same author also points out that the Holy See no longer speaks of Dialog Mass as being contrary to existing usage, because that is not now the case.[27]

Genoa's Cardinal-Archbishop felt that Dialog Mass was not only permissible but that it was *incumbent on priestly zeal* to promote it. These words to his priests lose nothing of their correctness in that they anticipated by some months the papal document we have just cited. "It is the duty of priests," he says, "to associate the faithful with the active celebration of the divine Mysteries, and not merely content themselves with silent assistance. The recitation of the rosary, morning prayers, acts of faith, etc., are good things. But it is a better thing for the people to join their voice with that of the server and priest at the altar."[28]

From all of which it will be clear, we trust, that the situation described by a visitor to Italy last year, is in fullest accord with the mind of our mother the Church: "You may still hear the rosary said during Mass, but you hear it much less often than formerly . . . It is by no means rare to hear the congregation making the responses."[29]

[26] *Hanssens*, 58*.
[27] *Hanssens*, 64*.
[28] Cardinal Minoretti, cf. *Orate Fratres*, IX, 2 (December 29, 1934), 74.
[29] Nesta de Robeck, *Tablet* (London) excerpted in *Orate Fratres*, XIV, 11 (September 29, 1940), 523.

CHAPTER V

ENCIRCLING THE GLOBE[1]

"The part of the people in solemn public worship of the Catholic Church," says His Eminence Cardinal Hinsley, "is not that of passive spectators. On the contrary, at Mass, priest and people, with Christ at our head, join in a united oblation in which every individual should share. All over the world, from far off Africa to our own shores, Almighty God in His providence is bringing us to a fuller realization of what our worship demands of us, a deeper sense of what it means to be an active member of the Mystical Body of Christ. United with Christ our Saviour, and with each other, in the solemn Sacrifice and prayer of the sacred liturgy, the faithful will find the surest means of personal sanctification and spiritual growth."[2]   Of course the Dialog Mass is only *one* manifestation of this Catholic worship, new style, but it is a manifestation that is found to be catholic. Therein lies our assurance : *securus iudicat orbis terrarum.* This chapter will sketch in outline, not only hemisphere solidarity, but whole-sphere uniformity, so to speak, in the approval of this new manifestation of Catholicism we call the Dialog Mass.

[1] This chapter embodies some items appearing in other contexts in my *Men at Work at Worship* (New York: Longmans, Green and Co., 1940): these are quoted with permission, and that book is referred to subsequently as *Men.*

[2] A. Cardinal Hinsley, Foreword, *The Mass and the Life of Prayer,* by A. Thorold (New York: Sheed & Ward, 1939), ix, x: quoted with permission.

I.— *The Americas*

To begin then in our New World surroundings. The penetration of the Dialog Mass into the frozen reaches of Alaska is enthusiastically chronicled by the Coadjutor Vicar Apostolic, Most Reverend Walter J. Fitzgerald, S.J., on another page of this book.[3]

And Canada? Under the patronage of Archbishop William Forbes, of Ottawa, the Dominion held its first Liturgical Week in 1931, at which the prelates present went on record to the effect : "Resolved, That the Dialog Mass be encouraged in educational institutions and religious communities."[4] Besides a letter from the office of His Eminence, Cardinal Villeneuve, giving the directions for Dialog Mass for Quebec, I have before me now reports of the Dialog Mass in churches and schools and religious houses in the metropolitan cities of Edmonton, Montreal, Ottawa, Regina, St. Boniface, Toronto, and the episcopal city of London. These emanate from diocesan priests, Oblates, Jesuits, Christian Brothers; Dominican, Notre Dame and Ursuline Sisters; Sisters of St. Joseph, Grey Nuns, Religious of the Sacred Heart.

Our neighboring republic to the South observed a nation-wide, papally-approved year of Liturgy in 1939. In the documentation arising therefrom one sees numerous episcopal exhortations to the use of the missal. The one clear item of evidence for episcopal initiative in the spread of the Dialog Mass is furnished in a letter from His Excellency Bishop Schlarman, to the effect that the Most Reverend Pedro Vera y Zunia, Archbishop of Puebla, "insists on the daily *Missa Reci-*

[3] Cf. p. 117.
[4] *Lefebvre*, 193.

tata in his seminary." There is, too, that little bit of Mexico *in partibus infidelium Americanorum,* so to speak, the Montezuma Seminary, at Las Vegas, New Mexico. It is most reliably reported that Dialog Mass has recently been given warm welcome there.

Before going beyond the Gulf, let us cast a glance at the Bahamas and Jamaica. Of the Bahamas a priest from the United States, Reverend Luke Fink, O.S.B., wrote recently in *Orate Fratres:*

"On my recent visit to the Bahama Islands . . . I had the deep satisfaction of witnessing a greater realization of the ideals of the liturgical movement than I had thought possible in our age—and certainly greater than any realization of which I know among the more favored congregations of our own country. . .

"Attendance at Mass in any of the mission chapels is like a revelation. . . The people take an active part in every Mass. If a low Mass, it is invariably a *Missa Recitata;* and the manner in which these simple, poor folk, some of them illiterate, recite the resonant Latin phrases is movingly edifying—and amazing! I remember one morning when I celebrated the six o'clock Mass. It was cold and rainy, and consequently only about three or four natives were present. . . In the circumstances, I did not think of a *Missa Recitata,* and therefore started the prayers at the foot of the altar in a low voice. But even these few would not be denied their privilege of active assistance. They answered heartily their '*Ad Deum qui laetificat . . .*' and so on, throughout the Mass, making up in volume what they lacked in numbers." [5]

[5] L. Fink, O.S.B., *Orate Fratres,* XV, 7 (May 18, 1941), 331-42: quoted with permission.

Jamaica on the old Spanish Main now finds the Dialog Mass regularly offered in the cathedral and Jesuit college chapel in Kingston, at Greenwich, Holy Cross, Linstead, Montego Bay, St. George's, Savanna la Mar, Spanish Town, in towns and in the 'bush.' Of the fourteen major mission stations of the Vicariate, nine now have Dialog Mass in one form or another. It was a young men's club, we are informed, that had Dialog Mass begun in the Kingston Cathedral, where-upon two of the cathedral sodalities started observing their monthly reunion with Dialog Mass. The hope has been expressed that all low Masses at the cathedral will come to be in dialog form. Thanks to the zeal of Reverend John P. Sullivan, S.J., *Catholic Opinion,* published in Kingston, carries crusading articles on Dialog Mass, from one of which we quote this climactic snatch : "Everywhere within the last decade or so, everywhere slowly but surely the hitherto silent, speechless Mystical Body of Christ is becoming vocal, articulate. I had almost said vociferous, as it approaches more closely the altar of Sacrifice, as it becomes more keenly conscious of . . . the dialog form of the Mass." [6]

If the Jamaican Caribs thrill to the discovery of the Dialog Mass, none the less so do their cousins in British Honduras, Central America, whence this letter recently came from the Vicar Apostolic in Belize :

"Dear Reverend Father : The Dialog Mass in this colony is spreading and is bringing the people to a gradual realization of what they have been losing by assisting at the Mass without taking active part in the Holy Sacrifice. The Men's Sodality, the Rosary So-

[6] *Catholic Opinion,* XLV, 3 (September, 1940), 39, 40: quoted with permission.

ciety, the boys of St. John's College and the girls of St. Catherine's High School are all taking up the study of the Mass with enthusiasm. Already the boys and girls have had Dialog Mass and have given us evidence of how beautifully it can be done.

"I do not know of any better means for promoting the knowledge and devotion necessary for the proper assisting at the holy Sacrifice. May its use increase and spread for the greater glory of our Heavenly Father.

"Devotedly in Our Lord . . ."

Not far from the mouth of the silvery Plata, in Florida, Uruguay, His Excellency Bishop Miguel Paternain, C.SS.R., bishop of Florida-Melo, held a diocesan Liturgical Week in the late fall of 1940, about which he was gracious enough to inform me : "During the Liturgical Week we had Dialog Mass daily except on Saturday and Sunday. A Benedictine father in charge of the program acted as leader at the Dialog Mass. . . Convinced as I was that Dialog Mass would contribute in no small way to increase the participation of the faithful in the holy Sacrifice, I have been at pains to introduce it widely into my diocese. . . For lack of a suitable director we are able to have Dialog Mass here only from time to time. At these the people answer with the acolytes and also recite the parts that are chanted by the choir at High Mass. . . God bless the apostolic work in the fostering of the sacred liturgy."

Over the Andes from Florida is Chile, stretching its twenty-six hundred miles of length over a coastal strip, at one place as narrow as eight miles, never more than two-hundred-and-twenty miles across. In that area dwell four and one half million people, organized into seventeen ecclesiastical jurisdictions. The prelates of all Chile, archbishops, bishops and vicars apostolic, put out a joint pastoral for the Lent of 1937, in which they dealt with Dialog Mass in a setting that is as solemn as its manner is direct and forthright. The pertinent passages are as follows:

"The fulness of the priesthood conferred on us by episcopal consecration binds us to teach the faithful how they should render to God the homage which is His due, an obligation which we should consider the chief duty of our ministry. . .

"Now the homage rendered to God by the church is one and the same homage rendered to God by the whole Catholic organism, the Mystical Body of Christ; so much so that every one of the faithful, provided he is not separated from the love of Christ, is a living and efficient participant in the liturgical acts of the Church. This participation, however, to be complete and profitable, must be understood by the faithful. . .

"The participation becomes more intense, the more closely the faithful follow the priest at Mass, reciting in dialog with him those parts of the Mass in which they are supposed to take a specially active part. Such parts are the prayers at the foot of the altar, the *Gloria, Credo, Sanctus, Benedictus* and *Agnus Dei.* Conformably to the regulations of the Holy See,* we authorize this form of piety, providing it will not be the occasion of distraction, and we recommend it especially for colleges and mass-meetings of Catholic Action. But this must not be practiced without due reverence and accuracy. . ." 7

Thus this section of our survey has shown us the

* Response to Cardinal Archbishop of Genoa, 1935.
7 *Men,* 49, 50.

Dialog Mass spreading under episcopal incentive and direction from the Yukon on the Arctic to the Straits of Magellan and Tierra del Fuego.

II. — Europe

Belgium has always enjoyed a primacy of honor in the use of the Dialog Mass, so there is justice in adducing, as first European witness in this chapter, His Eminence Cardinal Von Roey, Primate of that nation. At a Liturgical Week in historic old Nivelles, the Cardinal-Archbishop of Malines thus voiced his conviction of the important role of the liturgical movement: "I have a profound impression that the Holy Spirit is working in souls and that He is raising up everywhere a magnificent effort towards good. The liturgy is particularly important, for it is not a mere segment, apart and autonomous, of Catholic life. No, it is to pervade everything. It has a great role to play and in every domain of Christian life: parishes, schools, Catholic Action, social work."[8] That the Cardinal and his associates in the Belgian hierarchy interpret such ideas as applying in the concrete to the Dialog Mass is seen in this excerpt from *The Acts and Decrees of the Fifth Provincial Council of Malines,* 1937:

"For securing this spiritual unification, that active external participation will be of great help by which the faithful are present at the function not 'as detached and silent spectators,' but either by chanting or by praying 'they mingle their voices alternately with the priest and choir, as is prescribed.' "[9]

For the witness of Britain in this sketch we are privi

[8] Cardinal Von Roey: *cf. Orate Fratres,* XIV, 7 (May 12, 1940), 330 quoted with permission.
[9] Cf. *Men,* 10.

leged to print here a letter, reflecting all those qual-
ities that have builded England's greatness, from the
pen of England's war-time Primate, Arthur Cardinal
Hinsley:

"LONDON, *March* 19, 1941.

"Dear Father Ellard: The *Missa Dialogata* has not,
as far as I am aware, been officially approved by the
hierarchy of England and Wales, neither has it been
made the subject of disapproval.

"Personally I give my hearty approval to the *Missa
Dialogata* whenever it can be practiced with reverence.
Like all good things the *Missa Dialogata* may degen-
erate into abuse, that is to say, if not safeguarded
against mere noisy answering by a large congregation.
Therefore, We in this Archdiocese of Westminster require that leave be asked and given for the introduction of the *Missa Dialogata* in any parish, and there
should be a leader and controller of the answering by
the body of the Faithful attending Mass.

"We know that in the great central Act of worship,
which is the Sacrifice of the Mass, each one present can
and ought to unite with the High Priest and Victim
of the altar.   This is a silent union of our hearts with
the Sacred Heart of Jesus in the representation of the
Supreme Offering of Calvary.   At the moment of
Consecration our souls long to be undisturbed.   In
the preparatory prayers and the prayers of thanksgiving, in the *Gloria* and *Credo* especially, we want to be
able to say with St. Paul, 'I will pray with my spirit,
I will pray also with the understanding: I will sing
with the spirit, I will sing also with the understanding.'   Mere formalism and passive attendance at Mass
lead to indifference.   Our people must be induced to
learn the meaning of the Mass and the prayers which

precede or follow the great Act. Therefore Pius X so urgently insisted on corporate worship, and on the intelligent assistance of the Faithful. This is the meaning of the *Missa Dialogata,* as I understand it. But its introduction should be effected by gradual training of the people, who ought to learn the sense of the words used, and its continuance should be safeguarded, lest it become a distraction rather than a means of edification.

"With a blessing . . ."

Two years ago the writer had a communication from another Prince of the Church, the Primate of All Ireland, who wrote, among other things : "Here and there [in Ireland] the Dialogue Mass is being tried. About a year ago I authorized one of my own priests to attempt this Dialogue Mass, and I am awaiting a report from him, as to how the experiment has succeeded." At this time Cardinal MacRory, with that charm that has won him hosts of friends, shares with us a statement from the priest in question.

April 2, 1941.

"Dear Father Ellard : On receipt of your letter I wrote to Father MacIvor, C.C., and received the enclosed statement from him this morning. I am sorry I cannot give more help.

"Yours very faithfully, [etc.],

STATEMENT

" 'The practice of the Dialogue Mass has as yet barely made its first timid appearance in this country ; and indeed it is still rare enough to see efforts of a purposeful, and comprehensive kind at active corporate wor-

A. Cardinal Hinsley
Archbishop of Westminster

"I give my hearty approval to the *Missa Dialogata*"

ship. Some of the activities of the liturgical movement are here, but it has not as yet revealed to us its depths. . . .

'There are no insuperable difficulties in the way of furthering the practice of the Dialogue Mass amongst us : On the contrary it is rendered easy by the living faith of the people which makes them readily responsive to every unfolding of the riches of religion. It is only necessary that prudent regard be had for present realities and that effort and procedure be conformable to the national temperament.

'This conclusion is confirmed for the writer, by the experience of certain modest efforts made a few years ago, with the results of which he had had no reason to be dissatisfied.

(Signed) DERMOT MacIVOR' "

His Excellency, the Bishop of Limoges, France, combines, in his fostering of Dialog Mass, example, exhortation and very careful instruction. When he first came to his See, late in 1938, he made a tour of its seventeen deaneries in as many days and met his clergy morning after morning in the celebration of a Dialog Mass. Therewith he also urged its adoption into all the parishes of the diocese.[10] Not content with this, the bishop issued not long afterwards, for the guidance of his clergy in following out his directives, a very detailed Instruction on the same subject. *The Bombay Examiner* gives the following digest of Bishop Rastouil's prescriptions :[11]

"The Instruction distinguishes three degrees in the participation of the laity:

[10] Cf. *Men,* 22.
[11] July 6, 1940, 420: quoted with permission.

(1) collective recitation of the server's answers, along with
the server ;
(2) in addition, the *Gloria, Credo, Sanctus* and *Agnus Dei,*
and
(3) in addition again, the *Confiteor* before Communion and
the *Domine non sum dignus.*

ADVANTAGES :

1. This practice always creates a lively interest ;
2. It makes the faithful come oftener to the Mass ;
3. It invites them to come closer to the sanctuary in order to
follow more easily ;
4. It multiplies the number of persons following the Mass in
a missal ;
5. It instructs pious souls ever more in the spiritual riches of
holy Mass ;
6. It fosters more numerous and more fervent Communions,
because Communion is better understood by a more active
participation in the whole divine Sacrifice.

CONDITIONS :

A. *On the part of the priest* :
1. Pronounce intelligibly and slowly those prayers which call
for an answer from the faithful.
2. Give the congregation time to answer.
3. Explain the Mass to them : theology, liturgy, practice.
4. Invite them to procure a daily missal and help them to
procure one.
5. Teach them how to use a missal.
6. Provide them with an *Ordo* in the vernacular.
7. Every day indicate the Mass of the day.
8. Provide sufficient light for reading.
B. *On the part of the faithful* :
1. Have a daily missal and learn how to use it.
2. Learn the answers of the Mass by reading them with the
others.
3. Take a place in front close to the sanctuary.
4. Be careful to answer at the same time as the others.

Who would deny that Bishop Rastouil has the Gallic gift for clear and precise direction?

From Germany in mid-War comes little news not directly concerned with the cataclysmic conflict: one such item, however, bears directly on our subject-matter — episcopal action in spreading the Dialog Mass. We give the note as it appeared in *America,* having failed to find access to the issue of *Schoenere Zukunft,* mentioned as its source: "According to *Schoenere Zukunft,* German Catholic weekly, the German Bishops, at last year's conference at Fulda, passed a resolution that they would themselves take the lead in the liturgical movement in Germany. A special report was drawn up on liturgical questions, whose treatment was entrusted to Bishop Stohr of Mainz and Bishop Simon Konrad Landersdorfer of Passau. Bishop Landersdorfer particularly urged the participation of the faithful in liturgical services, the celebration of the community or Dialog Mass and liturgical evening prayers." [12] This is of a piece with the previous acts of many German Ordinaries, like Cardinal Schulte of Cologne, Cardinal Faulhaber of Munich, William Berning, Archbishop of Osnabrück, Michael Rackl, Bishop of Eichstaedt, Michael Buchberger, Bishop of Ratisbon, all of whom had previously urged Dialog Mass on their diocesans. The great-spirited Cardinal of Munich will be allowed a characteristic quotation from a conference to his priests: "The most precious heritage of the Savior, holy Mass, is again esteemed more and more in its relation to Christian living even by the laity, and is being again co-offered. The sacrificing priest, now as in Christian antiquity, has a sacrificing community, a

[12] *America,* LXIV, 20 (Feb. 22, 1941), 536.

plebs sancta Dei, behind him, which greets his *Orate Fratres* with a ready and fervent *Suscipiat Dominus.* The genuine community of worship would seem to wish to arise anew. I hear on all sides from the laity the most cordial thanks for this work so full of blessings already accomplished in many churches, particularly in Munich itself, by the reverend clergy, to re-establish the Christian community in common worship." [13]

There used to be a land called Austria, a beautiful home of tradition and culture, one singularly dear to Catholics the whole world over. From that land of eclipse one may here quote two items. The one looks to the future : it is a decree of the 1933 Diocesan Synod of Gurk-Klagenfurt : "Within the limits prescribed by the Church, the faithful shall be instructed in and attracted to active participation in the Sacrifice of the Mass." [14] The second looks both forward and backward : it is an address to his clergy by Ignatz Cardinal Innitzer after the great Catholic Congress (*Katholikentag*) of October, 1933. Says His Eminence :

"The Catholic Congress, in its most beautiful function at Schoenbrunn . . . teaches us also where and how we should start to foster an increased cultivation of Catholic life. The holy Sacrifice, as the true communal public worship, beautifully and worthily celebrated, with the greatest possible active participation of the people, dare no longer be considered a dream or a wish.

"Schoenbrunn teaches us that our people are ready

---

[13] *Bibel und Liturgie,* IX (1934-35), 43. This item, and several others in this series were furnished me by Dom Godfrey Diekmann, O.S.B., Editor of *Orate Fratres.* In grateful acknowledgment the items are marked with the notation *Diekmann.*

[14] *Bibel und Liturgie,* VIII (1933-34), 322 : *Diekmann.*

for that genuine liturgical celebration. The venture of a Dialog Mass with song (*Betsingmesse*) celebrated by 250,000 people without prior knowledge or practice, demolishes all the objections that heretofore were advanced against the introduction of such communal celebrations.

"It is my most earnest wish that in all parish churches and in the [non-parochial] churches of the religious orders of the Archdiocese the responsible authorities take care to have such a communal Mass at least once a month." [15]

The Primate of Poland, August Cardinal Hlond, who has witnessed and witnessed to such indescribable horrors in recent times, once knew much happier days, such as he described in a Pastoral: "How full of meaning it is and how touching it is to see in those parishes having a flourishing spiritual life the parishioners crowding around the celebrant during the holy Sacrifice. Not as onlookers or silent spectators do these people share in the Mass. In such parishes the faithful understand the structure of the Mass, know its every part, unite themselves with the priest, take an intimate role with the priest in the liturgy and live it!" [16] Doubtless God had so strengthened Poland for what has come!

Czechoslovakia, as a geographical term, was always hard to handle; the nation thus called had a short-lived existence, but Prague on the Moldau has roots centuries deep in our civilization. Prague's Cardinal-Archbishop, Karl Kasper, on various occasions promoted the Dialog Mass by himself officiating at its celebration, as, for instance during Liturgical Week, Oc-

[15] *Bibel und Liturgie*, VIII (1933-34), 63 *sqq.: Diekmann.*
[16] *Bibel und Liturgie*, VII (1932-33), 535 *sqq.: Diekmann.*

tober, 1933.[17]   A participant in the 1935 Catholic
Congress at Prague wrote as follows : "On June 28th
we celebrated Dialog Mass. . . . Softly at first, then
louder and with more assurance, we all answered the
prayers with the celebrant. The Archbishop of
Prague, Cardinal Kasper, himself came to take part in
the communal celebration."[18]

The late Joseph Ambuehl (†1936), Bishop of Basle
and Lugano, more than once dealt with Dialog Mass in
his Lenten Pastorals.   From his last such message to
his flock let us listen to this passage :

"God be thanked that we again enjoy a most promising indication of general betterment in our age in
the liturgical movement. . . . Its aim is to bind the
people ever closer to the priest celebrating at the altar,
to bring the people to a communal celebration of the
holy Mysteries, to make public worship really the
people's affair in which all co-sacrifice and pray with
the priest.   The Church herself urges this communal
praying, inasmuch as she directs the priest again and
again to turn to the people with the words, 'Dominus
vobiscum,' and addresses her invitation, 'Sursum
corda,' in the plural number, and so wishes it to be
answered by the entire congregation, 'Habemus ad
Dominum,' . . . Such a people, such a community,
that Sunday after Sunday gathers around its parish
altar for social prayer, social Sacrifice, and the reception of the Bread of Angels, which the loving Lord
bestows on us, — such a community will gladly break
its bread in Christlike fraternal love with the poor and
needy of the community."[19]

[17] Bibel und Liturgie, VII (1932-33), 532: Diekmann.
[18] Bibel und Liturgie, IX (1934-35), 468: Diekmann.
[19] Bibel und Liturgie, X (1935-36), 333-34: ibid., VIII (1933-34), 231:
Diekmann.

The writer has already presented to the public data supplied us by the headquarters of *De Rebus Hispaniae*, Spanish Catholic Action center at Burgos, among other sources, on the rapid spread of Dialog Mass in both civil and military life in Spain in recent times.[20] His Eminence, Cardinal Gomá y Tomás, Primate of Spain, has himself recently published a book on the social values of worship, but the mishaps of war-time transportation prevent us, thus far, from knowing in just what terms the Primate deals with Dialog Mass.

Spain's Iberian partner, Portugal, has enjoyed a liturgical, as well as an economic and social springtime for some years now. It was through the initiative of the Cardinal Patriarch of Lisbon, E. G. Cerejeira, that the seminary of Olivias saw a Gregorian Week, 1934, at which prelates and priests of the entire nation were present. An upshot of this was that the assembled bishops (Portugal has a hierarchy of fifteen members), established a National Commission with representation in each diocese, for the promotion of the liturgical movement. At the celebrations themselves, the people took part in the Masses, now in Gregorian song, now in the form of Dialog Mass, "as is recommended in the prescriptions of the liturgical and parochial action" of the Commission.[21]

Of Italy's part in the worldwide spread of the Dialog Mass by hierarchical direction there was fuller discussion in a previous chapter. Of the example of Pope Pius XI, and under him in Rome, of him who is now our Apostolic Delegate, Most Reverend Archbishop A. M. Cicognani, of Cardinals such as Ildefonso Schuster

20 *Men,* 27.
21 *Bibel und Liturgie,* IX (1934-35), 470: *Diekmann.*

at Milan, or the late Carlo Minoretti at Genoa, of the corporate action of the Lombard and Ligurian bishops, it is sufficient in this place to refer to what has been said previously. The Italian episcopate, in fostering Dialog Mass, was thinking 'from Rome outwards,' was thinking with the Roman heart.

Austria (that was), Belgium, Czechoslovakia, England, France, Germany, Ireland, Italy, Poland, Portugal, Spain, Switzerland — what are these but the outposts of that Rome our fathers knew as Christendom, all sharing in the heritage of that Rome, of which, in Dante's phrase, Christ Himself was a Roman.

III — In The Pacific and in Asia

Catholicism in the Hawaiian Islands has just received the papal recognition of being elevated to the rank of an episcopal see, and integrated into the regular hierarchy as a suffragan of San Francisco. In a very true sense Damien's Molokai is now an American parish! When His Excellency, Bishop J. J. Sweeney, reached Honolulu, he found Dialog Mass celebrated all Sundays and weekdays in at least two places in that city, at the Sacred Heart Church and the Maryknoll School.

"For two years now," ran a letter to *Orate Fratres* from the Very Reverend K. H. Kelly, V.F., in 1939, in Ayr, Diocese of Sale, Australia, "we have been having the Dialog Mass in the schools and colleges here. I should explain that I am Director of Education and have taken all the rules of the Mass from and have accepted the authority of *Orate Fratres* for all that I have introduced into the schools.

"It has been a wondrous blessing and has the warm admiration and approval of the Bishop [Most Reverend Richard Ryan, C.M.]. Many other bishops are interested, as well as other directors of education. We were the first to use it, and now recently in Melbourne the director there introduced it at the annual rally of the Catholic Youth. It looks as though the Dialog Mass may come into its own in many parts of Australia, and to a large extent this is the result of your work in *Orate Fratres*." [22]

The metropolitan of Manila, occupying a see that dates from 1579, stands at the head of the most solidly Catholic grouping in the whole Orient. The present Archbishop, Most Reverend Michael O'Doherty, has had Dialog Mass weekly for over five years in his San José Seminary, Balintawah, Rizal. Then, too, the college in connection with the San Beda Abbey, and the Ateneo College, under the Jesuits, have also now provided Dialog Mass for the young Philippinos. There were recently, under Benedictine auspices, radio talks on the Dialog Mass, as well as an article in *The Philippine Commonweal*, which in reporting America's Liturgical Week last October, laid stress on the desire there expressed for "the universal adoption of the Dialog Mass at one service on Sunday." [23] These are all

---

[22] Cf. *Men*, 145.

[23] I owe this information to Pedro Verceles, S.J., at one time connected with the Seminary mentioned. He praised in particular the work of Coleman A. Daily, S.J. The article referred to is "The Living Parish," by J. M. Urgell, O.S.B., *The Philippine Commonweal*, XI, 279 (March 8, 1941), 8. It is to the pen of the same Father Daily that I owe the following details about the Dialog Mass and the use of the Missal in the Ateneo de Manila:

THE LOG OF DIALOG MASS AT THE ATENEO DE MANILA

1938. No doubt the first enthusiasm for the Dialog Mass was inspired by the various and numerous articles in the Catholic magazines received at the Ateneo. Foremost among the devotees of this practice was Father William Dow, S.J. . . He repeatedly urged in his religion classes a

indications, I believe, that the Dialog Mass in the Islands is a quite recent addition to a Catholicism older by centuries than our own.

Data at hand on the status of the Dialog Mass in Japan is sparse but in the same vein as elsewhere. Missionaries' reports indicate their use of Dialog Mass with episcopal commendation. "In 1936," writes Gustav Voss, S.J., sometime faculty member of the Catholic University, Tokyo, "after the first Japanese translation of the Roman missal had been published, our Catholic Students' Guild inaugurated the custom of having Dialog Mass once a month in our University chapel. Many members of the hierarchy honored the students by celebrating this Mass for them. Among

greater devotion to the Mass and emphasized the use of the Missal at Mass. The interest gradually grew among the Jesuit scholastics.

The first step in the practical order was the mimeographing of copies of the responses at Mass. These were used at intervals by the boarders at Mass. A large number of the Queen's Work booklet, *Community Mass*, was sold. About twenty-five missals were bought locally by the students.

1939. The enthusiasm for the deeper appreciation of the Mass was universal among the students. Mass was explained during religion classes and students were urged to purchase missals. Dialog Mass was tried four or five times a month during this year. The students' interest was very evident. The mimeographed copies of the responses were still being used, but due to their cumbrousness and the noise in turning the pages, these copies were discarded. By the end of that year approximately one hundred boys had purchased missals.

1940. Prior to the reopening of classes, in the Sodality program September was designated as Missal Month. Sodality moderators during that month agreed to concentrate on: 1) Teaching the Dialog Mass; 2) The sale of missals; 3) Preparations for the Field Mass in December, a Dialog Mass for the entire student body. Our order was placed for 300 missals, an order which the agent raised to 500, the entire stock of which was sold among the students. Intensive training for the public Dialog Mass was carried on by the various Sodality prefects. After two weeks' intensive training, Mass was held in the Students' Chapel, and of course proved a huge success. . . . Two thousand students and alumni attended the Field Mass, and to insure coordinaton in the responses a public address system was constructed on the campus. The Mass was a tremendous success and impressed the Alumni.

Other colleges heard about our success and began a drive for the use of Dialog Mass. . .

1941. Enthusiasm for the missal and for the Dialog Mass continues to grow. The Field Mass was repeated this year.

them were the Most Reverend Paul Marella, Papal Delegate to Japan ; the Most Reverend Tatsuo P. Doi, who had then recently been consecrated the first Japanese Archbishop of Tokyo, and the Rt. Reverend Msgr. A. Akira Ogihara, S.J., Apostolic Administrator of Hiroshima. This custom has continued for the past five years with ever-increasing success. One of the students commented on its missionary value in these terms : 'To my mind the *Missa Recitata* is one means, and a very effective one, to interest the non-Catholics in our religion. We show them that we actively participate in our worship, a practice altogether foreign to them, but which they find inspiring.' " [24]

Details are recorded from time to time in the mission publications. Thus, Father Rudolf Kellner, O.F.M., narrates in the *Phos Christou* how his *'pusillus grex'* of twenty-five adults at Rumoi, Hokkaido, Japan, took to the Dialog Mass even at the cost of mastering the Latin pronunciation. "You should hear with what pride my simple Christians make the Latin responses, clearly and with perfect assurance." [25] A similar state of affairs is reported of the Japanese in Muroran, under the leadership of Father Titus Ziegler, O.F.M.

From the journal just quoted one learns of the penetration of the Dialog Mass into Chosen (Korea). From a long account by Dom Fabian Damm, O.S.B., on Dialog Mass in Genzan, I take note that the writer is at pains to correct the notion that Dialog Mass means the end of singing at low Mass. He states :

"The Asiatic, at least, the Korean, wants variety, and gets variety, and so we sing :

---

[24] Memorandum made for the author, April, 1941.
[25] *Phos Christou*, No. 33, September, 1938.

"(1) At the priest's entrance . . . and during the prayers at the foot of the altar (which originally were not said at the altar), we sing up to the *Confiteor*, which is recited aloud ;

"(2) After the Offering of the chalice to the beginning of the Preface ;

"(3) During the distribution of Holy Communion, which here takes at least ten minutes on Sundays. . . . Of course, it goes without saying that the hymns are appropriate for the respective parts of the Mass ;

"(4) Finally, we sing once more after the blessing . . ." [26]

The quasi-Dialog Mass as found in China, and referred to by The First Plenary Council of China, Shanghai (1924) as "the prayers which are wont to be recited by all the faithful jointly in the churches," has already been dealt with by the writer in some detail.[27] Among the prayers thus said by the faithful, men on one side alternating with the women on the other, are the *Confiteor, Kyrie, Gloria* and *Credo,* so that it is hardly excessive to say that the Chinese have a super-Dialog Mass erected on the longest and hardest elements of the more *responsive* dialog known elsewhere.

The Diocese of Hyderabad, India, is in the Ecclesiastical Province of Madras, its bishop since 1924 being Dionigi Vismara. In His Excellency's Lenten Pastoral for 1939 the Roman prohibition against the loud recitation of the Canon suggested this passage : "A priest or catechist during the Mass explains (very briefly) what is going on, especially the prayers of the

---

[26] Compare the author's suggestions, independently arrived at, on pages 180 *sqq.*
[27] *Men*, 246-50.

Canon, which are not allowed to be said in an audible voice, and leads the actions and prayers of the people. As to the other parts of the Mass, the faithful assisting may well answer the priest's prayers with the server, and also recite the *Gloria, Credo, Sanctus* and *Agnus Dei.*" [28]

Africa? It remains in this matter the dark continent. Evidence is superabundant as to the flourishing condition of Gregorian plainsong in the African missions, but in the materials at my present disposal I find no mention of Dialog Mass.

*

* *

The Americas, Europe, Asia, Australasia, all have felt the initiative of the hierarchy in fostering Dialog Mass, a ready and easy form of that communal prayer regarded as so necessary by Pope Pius XI : "A need of our times," he told a pilgrim group in 1929, "is social, or communal prayer, to be voiced under the guidance of the pastors in enacting the solemn functions of the liturgy. This alternating of prayers will be of the greatest assistance in banishing the numberless evils which disturb the minds of the faithful in our age, and especially in overcoming the snares and dangers which threaten to undermine the sincerity of the faith." [29]

Securus iudicat orbis terrarum.

[28] *Men,* 135.
[29] Latin text, of *Ephemerides Liturgicae,* XLIV, 1 (Jan.-Feb., 1930), 3, 4.

CHAPTER VI

TWENTY-FIVE AMERICAN BISHOPS, ONE HUNDRED SEES

Several American publishers were asked in 1938 about arranging the missals on their lists for use at Dialog Mass; none at that time showed interest. When in 1940 Father Stedman issued the nationally known *My Sunday Missal,* with such an arrangement for Dialog Mass, he could state that the edition "goes forth with the prayer of many bishops and priests that the 'Dialog' or 'Community' Mass may once again become the universal way for the faithful to recite the 'Ordinary.'" [1] Thus, in the United States, the Dialog Mass, as something promoted by hierarchical authority, is but of yesterday. It is fortunate indeed that in a project so very recent, and one that the Holy See leaves entirely in the hands of each individual bishop, to adopt or not as he may see fit, we are already in a position to glimpse something of the results over the country as a whole. This is owing to a happy combination of circumstances.

Since 1926 American Sodality manuals have carried the direction: the bishop so permitting, the Sodalists' Mass should be a Dialog Mass.[2] Now, when the pro-

---

[1] J. F. Stedman, *My Sunday Missal,* Latin-English Edition, Also Dialogue Mass (Brooklyn, 1940), p. 34. *The Leaflet Missal,* it must be added, has since 1930, indicated a distinction between parts properly said by the server and those historically said by the people. The *Saint Andrew Missal* has carried a Dialog Mass arrangement since 1936 in its English editions.

[2] *The Sodality Manual* (St. Louis: Queen's Work, 1926), 166; *The A.B.C. of Sodality Organization* (St. Louis, Queen's Work, 1927), 166.

ject of this book was first broached, the national office of the Sodality of the Blessed Virgin offered to submit a questionnaire on this use of the Dialog Mass to all the sodalities, and allied organizations, on its mailing lists. Thereupon sodality and youth directors in such parish and educational institutions as maintain relations with *The Queen's Work* received, and in some measure answered and returned, copies of an interrogatory framed as follows:

Questionnaire on Dialog Mass, January, 1941

.... Church .... (City) .... (Diocese)
.... (parish, private, diocesan *check which*)
.... College, conducted by ....

Dialog Mass is in use here: for children's Mass (check
       on Sundays: which)
       for adult congregation
      on weekdays: with what frequency . . ...

Parts said in whole or in part in English (check):

Parts said in whole or in part in Latin (check):

Parts said in whole or in part in English (check):	Parts said in whole or in part in Latin (check):
— 1.	— 1. Altar-boy responses
— 2. I confess	— 2. *Confiteor*
— 3. Lord have mercy (*Kyrie*)	— 3. *Kyrie eleison*
— 4. Glory to God	— 4. *Gloria in excelsis*
— 5. I believe	— 5. *Credo*
— 6. Offertory prayers	— 6.
— 7. Holy, holy, holy	— 7. *Sanctus, sanctus, sanctus*
— 8. Behold the Lamb of God	— 8. *Agnus Dei*
— 9. Lord Jesus Christ	— 9.
— 10. I confess	— 10. *Confiteor*
— 11. Lord, I am not worthy	— 11. *Domine non sum dignus*

Quite a few schools failed to name the locality in which their institutions were located, and so these returns

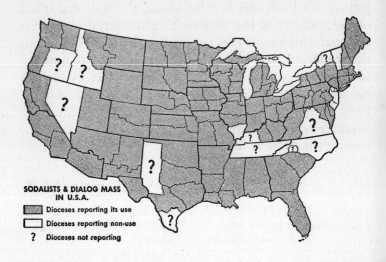

SODALISTS & DIALOG MASS
IN U.S.A.

▨ Dioceses reporting its use

☐ Dioceses reporting non-use

? Dioceses not reporting

were of no assistance in the study as a whole. Again, a good many duplications turned up, as in the familiar case of a high school group and college group in the same institution, and attending the same Mass, sending in separate reports. A careful attempt was made to exclude every such duplication. In very few instances in returns from the deep South it could not be ascertained, at first glance, whether one or two entities were involved, on questionnaires assigning different names for church and school. In the tabulations all *parochial schools* are merged with their respective parish churches, and do not appear in the lists. Thus, the only schools retained in the tabulation are central high schools, academies, private high schools, colleges, schools of nursing, universities. Returns were for the most part from the diocesan clergy. But Benedictines, Capuchins, Crosier Fathers, Dominicans, Jesuits, Holy Ghost Fathers, Marists, Oblates, Paulists, Precious

Blood Fathers, and Servites, if not other orders, too, were all represented, to say nothing of the teaching Brotherhoods and Sisterhoods. The final summation of this Sodality survey indicated results as follows:

Dioceses in which Dialog Mass is in use............... 91
Dioceses in which Dialog Mass is not allowed........ 2
Dioceses in which no information was supplied..... .. 20 [3]

At this stage of events it was felt that prior to publication of any of the data the bishops should be made acquainted with the survey. All Ordinaries, save those few known to have disallowed the Dialog Mass, were informed of the Sodality project just completed, and thus afforded an opportunity to add such information or comment as might severally please them. "I am much pleased that you are making a study on the Dialog Mass in our parishes and institutions," wrote Archbishop Stritch, and that this private, haphazard enquiry among Sodality affiliates might be supplemented in at least one case by an authoritative survey, he undertook such an investigation covering the entire Archdiocese of Chicago, America's most populous single jurisdiction. In somewhat similar fashion Bishop A. J. McGavick of LaCrosse, through his Auxiliary, Most Reverend W. R. Griffin, instituted a survey of the 158 churches of his diocese. Of the schools and institutions in his diocese Bishop McGavick wrote: "Bishop [Griffin] did not send cards to schools or institutions, as we know that all these use the Dialog Mass." These two surveys of the respective territories of the Ordinaries of Chicago and LaCrosse will be presented elsewhere in this volume. The result to date of the general survey gives this picture:

[3] In this listing, the Dioceses of the Oriental Rite, the Military Ordinariate, and the Diocese of Honolulu were not included.

Not the least interest attaching to the statements of the hierarchy is the range of ideas covered by them. Their Excellencies' letters will be quoted in fuller form below; here salient features are excerpted. The fundamental question of propriety and papal approbation is stated with lapidary precision in the phrases of Archbishop Stritch in a statement issued in June, 1940:

"This Missa Recitata, concerning which the S. C. R. explicitly legislated, and as it is universally celebrated, consists in its minimum form, in the congregation joining the server in his responses; in its more expanded form, also explicitly approved, the congregation, besides joining the server in the Latin responses, also recites with the celebrant the Ordinary parts of the Mass which in a *Missa Cantata* are intended to be sung by the congregation: i.e., the *Gloria, Credo, Sanctus* (and *Benedictus*), and *Agnus Dei.* Frequently added are the *Confiteor* and triple *Domine non sum dignus* immediately before the people's Communion."

The function and value of Dialog Mass as an instrument for effecting active participation on the part of the laity is well put by Archbishop Curley: "I have no hesitation in saying that the 'Dialogue System' is one of the best ways of bringing the people into closer contact with the priest who is offering up the holy Sacrifice, and at the same time make them realize what the Mass really is." Archbishop Rummel stated through his Chancellor, Very Reverend Carroll Badeaux, that he was "not convinced that this method is *uniformly*

M. J. CURLEY
Archbishop of Baltimore-Washington

"We shall do all we can to carry on this work"

desirable in the Archdiocese, but that he leaves it to the individual priests to adopt it on trial." The letter concludes with the view, "It is certainly a laudable objective to strive after."

Assuming this value as granted, Bishop E. V. O'Hara of Kansas City takes the long-range view as to the systematic and gradual introduction of Dialog Mass by starting now with those in high school. In an official direction preparatory to the recent Diocesan Eucharistic Congress in his diocese Bishop O'Hara stated:

"Since the 'dialogue' Mass is recognized as perhaps the most practical method of introducing popular participation in the liturgy of the Church, so ardently recommended by Pope Pius X and his successors in the Supreme Pontificate, we should look forward to encouraging it among the youth of all our parishes — and, in due time, to have our parish Mass on Sunday conducted in this manner. There is no thought of being hurried in this matter, for haste would probably result in defeating any permanent hope of achievement.

"We are, however, desirous of making a beginning in connection with our diocesan Eucharistic Congress, a feature of which will be the exemplification of how to conduct a 'dialogue' Mass by the Junior CYO groups of the Diocese. In preparation for this demonstration I am asking the pastors to have their Junior CYO groups become acquainted with the Community Mass during April."

Similarly the Vice-Chancellor of the Diocese of Altoona gives a new turn to *festina lente* in saying: "We intend to push the Dialog Mass gradually from this office and in our trips around the Diocese."

The year-by-year formation of the high school groups paves the way for the general adult use of Dialog Mass, in the opinion of Bishop Brady of Sioux Falls:

"To insure proper introduction, the Ordinary has urged that it be introduced at first only among the groups trained for the purpose — the nuns, children in school, etc. From this beginning, it is expected, as the children leave school and mingle with the adult congregation, to have a nucleus of trained and instructed persons who will be able to act as leaders, and around whom the other adults can rally in taking their part. . . . Wherever used, after proper introduction, it has stimulated interest in the liturgical life of the Church and given a new meaning to the Divine Sacrifice." That, too, would seem to be the supposition of Bishop Schulte's directions for the Diocese of Leavenworth: "We are heartily in favor of its use in religious houses and for the week-day Masses of children attending Catholic schools. We are in favor of its introduction into the parishes, when the reverend pastors find that the ground has been sufficiently prepared, so that it can be done intelligently, reverently, smoothly."

For heartiness in endorsing the Dialog Mass it is difficult to judge between the statements of Bishop Brady and those of his colleague, Bishop Winkelmann of Wichita. Says Bishop Brady: "In the Diocese of Sioux Falls the *Missa Recitata* or the Dialogue Mass is celebrated not only with the approval but with the recommendation of the Ordinary. It is held daily in many of the convent and hospital chapels: wherever possible, it is part of the school program."

To which comes as an echo from central Kansas: "We are not only in sympathy with this movement, but we are encouraging and introducing the Dialogue Mass wherever we can. I am confident that the time is most apropos to have the people come closer to the august Sacrifice and the liturgy of the Church, and to bring the liturgy to the people. I am convinced that much of this will have to be done by our devoted religious. I am, therefore, most anxious to see the Dialogue Mass used every day in our convents, and, if possible, also the Offertory procession. The novices and the young Sisters, who are preparing for their future work will, in consequence, go to the missions enthusiastic for the proper participation of the laity in the Sacred Mysteries."

With regard to the extent to which Dialog Mass has penetrated their respective dioceses there is the testimony of Bishop Peschges of Crookston that all his parishes having parochial schools have adopted it, with which we might balance the words of Bishop McGavick already quoted, to the effect that all his [private] schools and more than half his parishes now use Dialog Mass, or with those of Bishop Noll of Fort Wayne: "The Dialog Mass takes place daily in most convent chapels . . . at the cathedral . . . and I am certain in a very large number of churches."

The unifying effect of Dialog Mass is what Bishop Kelley of Oklahoma City-Tulsa chooses to stress in his endorsement: "It brings realization of the eternal greatness of the Holy Sacrifice to the people who assist at it. The Dialog Mass unites faithful and priest in the most sublime act of worship of all time. If 'it is the Mass that matters'—and it is, what better could be done than to make the Mass matter more and more to the faithful by giving them a more intimate knowledge of every part of it?"

While sharing these convictions of Bishop Kelley to the full, Bishop Alter of Toledo speaks a wise word of caution against too sudden and too sweeping changes: "I am not yet convinced that it is desirable to introduce the *Missa Recitata* on all days of the week or at all the Masses. Some people have found the procedure disturbing to their own private assistance at the Mass and in consequence I would favor the use of the Dialog Mass at some Masses only or from time to time rather than adopt it as a universal and continuous practice. As long as the practice is considered a privilege by the Sacred Congregation, I do not think it should take on the character of an obligation."

That Dialog Mass will spread from church to church by the experience of its own excellence is expressed in sentiments ranging from hope to conviction by several prelates. Bishop Peterson of Manchester is hopeful: "I trust that their example [Benedictine Fathers at Manchester] will be followed elsewhere."

Similarly Bishop G. O'Hara of Savannah-Atlanta: "This church (in charge of the Jesuit Fathers, by the way) is the only one in which we have the Dialog Mass. I should like very much to have this practice adopted universally throughout this Diocese."

For Bishop Scher of Monterey-Fresno it is more positive: states his chancellor-secretary: "The pastors have full permission to proceed in accord with their own judgment of local conditions. . . One parish contemplates the introduction of the method in the near future."

Bishop Toolen of Mobile has the certainty that comes of experience: "There are many parishes in the Diocese that are using the *Missa Recitata*, but I have made no statement in regard to it. Wherever they asked me if they might use it, I have encouraged them, but have not urged it upon them."

That the Dialog Mass fits into a proper place in the sequence of corporate worship practices is the opinion of Bishop Scher's neighbor, Bishop Budde of San Diego. Thus this bishop's secretary: "His Excellency does not think that the Dialog Mass would be practical as yet for this Diocese, as he has but recently introduced the use of the daily and Sunday Missal. In the future . . . we should be happy to have the opportunity to introduce the Dialog Mass in this Diocese."

Not all episcopal communications received are in favor of the Dialog Mass. Thus the Ordinary of Paterson states: "We are not giving permission for [the Dialog Mass]. It appears to me that, while greater participation of the laity is desirable at Mass, the Dialog Mass does not appear as a genuine contribution to the liturgical development, since it leads the people away more and more from High Mass, which is the one which the faithful should participate in." New Jersey has for years, as every one knows, been conspicuous in its thorough-going work in the teaching of plainchant to ever-greater groups of young people. It is natural that this program should be regarded as jeopardized by the introduction, at the half-way mark, of congregational recitation at low Mass.

However, that Dialog Mass can, and actually does, have the effect of stimulating congregational singing of the Mass is the testimony of a prelate on the opposite coast, Archbishop Howard of Portland. Says he: "In two parishes of this Archdiocese, to my knowledge, the *Missa Recitata* is used, at least once each week. . . You will be interested in knowing, no doubt, that in both of these parishes the Ordinary of the Mass is sung on a great many Sundays by the entire congregation at High Mass." So, too, that veteran promoter of the liturgical movement, Bishop Schlarman, of Peoria, in an address at the Regional Conference of the Confraternity of Christian Doctrine, Lincoln, April, 1941, argued in his own vigorous fashion that Dialog Mass for most of us must precede the sung Mass. "It is true," he says, "that both these Popes who urged the participation of the laity in the Mass had in their minds the *ideal* of Catholic worship, viz., a high Mass or *Missa Cantata*. Now there is also much sound sense in the old saying that a child must crawl before it can walk. Evidently, it is easier to *recite* the responses than to *sing* them. With that in mind, and at the same time trying to bring about a *more active participation* on the part of the people, some priests, with permission of their proper Bishop, have introduced the *Missa Recitata* or Dialog Mass, in which the faithful respond with the servers in a low Mass." Of his own diocese Bishop Schlarman said as far back as 1934: "While a [full] *Missa Recitata* cannot be considered as something that should be practiced exclusively, there will be but few parishes where something like it could not be done."

The language-barrier looks insuperable to Bishop Swint of Wheeling: "I have not been able to convince myself of the good of the Dialog Mass. I must confess that personally I have never witnessed one, and so what I have is from reading and hearing. But it seems to me that as long as the dialog is carried on in the Latin tongue, which the people do not understand, it is more of a distraction than a help. . . I am willing, however, to be convinced I am wrong."

This same language-barrier prompted Bishop Duffy

of Buffalo in 1937 to phrase an approbation of Dialog Mass in these words: "Our priests are authorized to organize the Dialog Mass when they are sure it will be done correctly, that is, with the uniform and regular pronunciation of the Latin words and with careful attention to the words of the priest so as not to delay him."

The dangers of externalism and formalism, for the general congregation, appear to Bishop Muench of Fargo too great to warrant his sanctioning Dialog Mass for general use. His approbation is limited as follows: "I would recommend the Dialog Mass be used for priests at their retreat or other gatherings whenever they assist at low Mass; for nuns and sisters in convents, at least on certain occasions; as well as for small groups of our educated laity. I do not recommend the Dialog Mass for general congregational use."

Thus every section of the country, almost every ecclesiastical province, is represented in these statements of hierarchical policy. These naturally send us to the detailed summaries of the Sodality survey. A bit of explanation will facilitate the reading of the tabulation. If all the pertinent data had been given in each case, the total number of places using Dialog Mass would equal the totals for frequency and for language, but incomplete data was recorded as received. Again, our picture on frequency is here most uneven, ranging all the way from once a year to seven days a week the whole year through. Under "English only" and "Latin only" are recorded sodalities marking their questionnaires respectively for English items only or for Latin items exclusively. By the English-Latin combination is meant the method wherein some prayers not said with the celebrant or server (such as prayers at the Offertory, or before Communion) are said in the vernacular, while all parts recited with either celebrant or server are in the official Latin. This form, it will be noted, is a two-to-one favorite among the sodalists.

PROVINCE OF BALTIMORE:

1. *Baltimore-Washington:*

"We have had the 'Dialogue Mass' in several churches of the Archdiocese of Baltimore and the people seemed very interested in it. Time and again I have appealed to my priests at their conferences to preach the Mass continuously. We have heard altogether too much about cosmos and other such things. What the people wish is to have a knowledge about the holy Sacrifice, what it is, how to attend Mass, and how to follow the priest during Mass. I have no hesitation in saying that the 'Dialogue System' is one of the best ways of bringing the people into closer contact with the priest who is offering up the Holy Sacrifice and at

	Sdys only	Wkdys only	Sdys & Wkdys	Engl. only	Latin only	Engl.-Latin
6 ch., Baltimore, Curtis Bay, Washington	4	1	1	3		3
13 coll., sch., Baltimore, Georgetown, Emmitsburg, Leonardstown, Mt. Washington, Washington	1	11	1	2	3	8
2. *Charleston:* sch., Aiken		1			1	
3. *Raleigh:* No information at hand						
4. *Richmond:* No information at hand						

the same time make them realize what the Mass really
is, apart from the choir, or any other phase, which may
be a distraction rather than a help.

"We shall do all we can in this Archdiocese to carry
on the work." — MICHAEL J. CURLEY, *Archbishop of
Baltimore and Washington.*

5. *Savannah-Atlanta:*

Survey afforded no information, but Bishop's letter
follows:

"It was only recently that I had personal experience
with respect to this form of assisting at Mass. I heard
it in the Sacred Heart Church, Augusta, Georgia, and
the idea pleased me very much. It was a real and active participation of the congregation in the Action of
the Mass. This church (in charge of the Jesuit
Fathers, by the way) is the only one in which we have
the Dialog Mass. I should like very much to have
this practice adopted universally throughout this Diocese." — GERALD P. O'HARA, *Bishop of Savannah-
Atlanta.*

	Sdys only	Wkdys only	Sdys & Wkdys	Engl. only	Latin only	Engl.-Latin
6. *St. Augustine:* ch., Jacksonville		I		I		

7. *Wheeling:*

"I beg to say that I have not yet been able to convince myself of the good of the Dialog Mass. I must
confess that personally I have never witnessed one, so
that what I have is from reading and hearing. But it
seems to me that as long as the dialog is carried on in

the Latin tongue, which the people do not understand, it is more of a distraction than a help. Some good prayers said during the Mass, or the use of an English missal, seems to me preferable. I am willing, however, to be convinced that I am wrong." — JOHN J. SWINT, *Bishop of Wheeling*.

	Sdys only	Wkdys only	Sdys & Wkdys	Engl. only	Latin only	Engl.-Latin
2 ch., Charleston, Wheeling		1	1		1	1
8. *Wilmington:* sch., Wilmington		1				1
9. *Belmont Abbacy-Nullius:* No information at hand						
	5	16	3	6	4	12

Summary:
Dioceses using DM, 6
  10 churches
  15 schools
No information   3

PROVINCE OF BOSTON:

	Sdys only	Wkdys only	Sdys & Wkdys	Engl. only	Latin only	Engl.-Latin
10. *Boston:* 4 ch., Boston, Fort Devens, Lowell	4			1	1	2
7 coll., sch., Boston, Arlington, Island Creek, Lenox, Stoneham, Weston	5	2		1	5	1
11. *Burlington:* Dialog Mass not permitted in this diocese						
12. *Fall River:* sch., Fall River		1				1[4]
13. *Hartford:* 3 ch., Waterbury, Willimantic			3	1		2

French-Latin combination.

14. *Manchester:*

Survey afforded no information, but Bishop's letter follows :

"As for the Dialog Mass I have had only one request for approbation to try it experimentally, which was gladly granted. This was in the parish of St. Raphael, conducted by the Benedictine Fathers, in the city of Manchester. I trust that their example will be followed elsewhere. Though not in a parish, it is well to add that at St. Anselm's College in Manchester the students have participated daily in the Dialog Mass during the past ten years." — JOHN B. PETERSON, *Bishop of Manchester.*

	Sdys only	Wkdys only	Sdys & Wkdys	Engl. only	Latin only	Engl.-Latin
15. *Portland:* 4 ch., Portland, Bangor, Fairfield 2 sch., Portland, Bangor		2	1 2	1	1	1
16. *Providence:* ch., Georgiaville	1			1		
17. *Springfield:* 2 sch., Chicopee, Worcester	1		1		1	1
	8	9	7	5	8	7

Summary:
Dioceses using DM, 7
 13 churches
 13 schools
Dioceses not using DM, 1

PROVINCE OF CHICAGO :

18. *Chicago:*

"This Missa Recitata concerning which the S.C.R. explicitly legislated, and as it is universally celebrated,

consists in its minimum form, in the congregation joining the server in his responses; in its more expanded
form, also explicitly approved, the congregation, besides joining the server in the Latin responses, also
recites with the celebrant the Ordinary parts of the
Mass which in a *Missa Cantata* are intended to be sung
by the congregation: i.e., the *Gloria, Credo, Sanctus*
(and *Benedictus*), and *Agnus Dei.* Frequently added
are the *Confiteor* and triple *Domine non sum dignus*
immediately before the people's Communion.

"This is the method approved according to the mind
of the Most Reverend Samuel A. Stritch, Archbishop
of Chicago."

	Sdys only	Wkdys only	Sdys & Wkdys	Engl. only	Latin only	Engl.-Latin
11 ch., Chicago, Cicero, Joliet, Momence 24 coll., sch., Chicago, Des Plaines, Joliet, Lake Forest, Techny, Wilmette[5]	7	1	2	3	4	3
19. *Belleville:* Dialog Mass not permitted in this diocese						

20. *Peoria:*

"I am happy to make report on the widespread practice of the *Missa Recitata* in the Diocese of Peoria.
The first *public Missa Recitata* was held in the Cathedral of Peoria on the occasion of the first Liturgical
Day, October 19, 1934. Some 700 Sisters and about
100 priests took part. That broke up the clouds of
scepticism concerning the Dialog Mass.

"For the last six years the Dialog Mass is celebrated

[5] These returns are to be compared with the official Archdiocesan survey
farther on, 94 churches, 50 educational institutions.

daily in the orphanage, in every hospital, Catholic institution, Motherhouse of Sisters, and Sisters' house where Mass is said. The Mass in the Bishop's chapel is always a *Missa Recitata*.

"Every First Friday I celebrate the *Missa Recitata* in the Cathedral with the pupils of Spalding Institute and the Academy of Our Lady. In my absence, Monsignor J. J. Leven, pastor of the Cathedral, takes my place. A number of priests have introduced the *Missa Recitata* on weekdays for the children.

"The 12 o'clock Mass on Sundays in the Cathedral is a *Missa Recitata*. The congregation does not yet respond to the prayers at the foot of the altar. A priest in the pulpit reads the Epistle and Gospel in English while the celebrant reads them at the altar. That gives more time for the sermon. The whole congregation reads the *Credo* in English. I am enclosing the form used in the Cathedral.[6]

	Sdys only	Wkdys only	Sdys & Wkdys	Engl. only	Latin only	Engl.-Latin
ch., Galesburg		1			1	
4 sch., Peoria, Galesburg, Navoo		4			4	
21. *Rockford:* 2 sch., Rockford, St. Charles		1	1		1	1
22. *Springfield:* 3 ch., Brussels, Effingham, Mt. Sterling	1		2		1	2
sch., Springfield		1				1
	8	32	5	3	17	25

Summary:
Dioceses using DM, 4
    14 churches
    31 colleges, schools
Dioceses not using DM, 1

[6] This form is printed at pages 207, 208.

"My Ordination Mass is always a *Missa Recitata* with a priest in the pulpit explaining the rite of ordination and reading many of the prayers in English. — Very sincerely yours in Christ," J. H. SCHLARMAN, *Bishop of Peoria.*

PROVINCE OF CINCINNATI:

	Sdys only	Wkdys only	Sdys & Wkdys	Engl. only	Latin only	Engl.-Latin
23. *Cincinnati:* 2 ch., Cincinnati, Xenia	1		1		2	
6 coll., sch., Cincinnati, Dayton, Westwood		5	1		3	3
24. *Cleveland:* 7 sch., Cleveland, Canton, East Euclid		7		1	2	4
25. *Columbus:* ch., Ironton		1				1
sch., New Lexington		1				1

26. *Fort Wayne:*

"The Dialog Mass takes place daily in most convent chapels, at Notre Dame, at St. Mary's, at Central Catholic High School, Fort Wayne; at St. Francis High

	Sdys only	Wkdys only	Sdys & Wkdys	Engl. only	Latin only	Engl.-Latin
Cath., 3 ch., Fort Wayne, Crown Point	2	1	1	2		
4 coll., sch., Fort Wayne, Holy Cross, Lafayette, Notre Dame, Tipton		2	3		1	3
27. *Indianapolis:* Cath., Indianapolis, 2 ch., Oldenburg, Vincennes		3		2		1
5 sch., Indianapolis, Terre Haute		4	1	1	2	2

School, Lafayette; at the Cathedral and St. Paul Churches, Fort Wayne, and I am certain in a very large number of churches of the Diocese." — J. F. NOLL, *Bishop of Fort Wayne.*

28. *Toledo:*

"In our Cathedral church, in several parishes and in various academies, the Dialog Mass or *Missa Recitata* has been made use of on various occasions. I have gladly given my approval whenever a petition has been submitted to me asking for this privilege.

"In my judgment when the congregation joins with the acolytes in reciting the responses of the Mass, there is created a sense of active participation in the Mass and certainly a better appreciation of its various parts. This active participation should normally increase the spiritual appreciation of the meaning of the Mass and increase the spirit of devotion.

"I am not yet convinced that it is desirable to introduce the *Missa Recitata* on all days of the week or at all of the Masses. . . . As long as the practice is considered a privilege by the Sacred Congregation, I do not think it should take on the character of an obligation." —KARL J. ALTER, *Bishop of Toledo.*

	Sdys only	Wkdys only	Sdys & Wkdys	Engl. only	Latin only	Engl.-Latin
Cath., 3 ch., Toledo, Fremont 3 sch., Toledo	2	3	2	1	1	2 3
	4	26	7	7	12	18

Summary:
  Dioceses approving DM, **6**
    13 churches
    26 coll., schools

PROVINCE OF DENVER:

	Sdys only	Wkdys only	Sdys & Wkdys	Engl. only	Latin only	Engl.-Latin
29. *Denver:* Cath., ch., Colorado Springs school, Boulder		2 1			1 1	1
30. *Cheyenne:* ch., Casper	1			1		
31. *Pueblo:* school, Pueblo			1	1		
	1	3	1	2	2	1

Summary:
Dioceses using DM, 3
3 churches, 2 schools

PROVINCE OF DETROIT:

	Sdys only	Wkdys only	Sdys & Wkdys	Engl. only	Latin only	Engl.-Latin
32. *Detroit:* 8 ch., Detroit, Adrian, Royal Oak 5 coll., sch., Detroit, Monroe	2	4	6 1	2	2 4	4 1
33. *Grand Rapids:* 5 ch., Grand Rapids, Cadillac, Ludington, Muskegan, Rosebush		1	4	1	1	3
34. *Lansing:* 2 ch., Lansing, Owosso, sch., Jackson City	1		1 1	1 1		1
35. *Marquette:* 3 ch., Escanaba, Laurium, Sault Ste. Marie	2		2			3
36. *Saginaw:* 4 ch., Saginaw, Merrill, Pinconning		2	2		1	3
	5	7	16	5	8	15

Summary:
Dioceses approving DM, 5
22 churches
6 colleges, schools

PROVINCE OF DUBUQUE:

	Sdys only	Wkdys only	Sdys & Wkdys	Engl. only	Latin only	Engl.-Latin
37. *Dubuque:*						
ch., Lansing		1		1		
5 coll., sch., Dubuque, Cedar Rapids, Stacyville	1	4		1	2	2
38. *Davenport:*						
Cath., 2 ch., Davenport, Clinton	2		1	1	1	1
sch., Davenport		1				1
39. *Des Moines:*						
ch., Des Moines		1	1			
sch., Des Moines		1				1
40. *Grand Island:*						
sch., Alliance		1		1		
41. *Lincoln:*						
2 ch., Beatrice, Dwight	2					2
42. *Omaha:*						
4 ch., Omaha, Columbus, Hartington, O'Neill	1	1	2		1	1
5 coll., sch., Omaha, O'Neill	1	4		2	1	2
43. *Sioux City:*						
12 ch., Sioux City, Algona, Ashton, Bode, Fort Dodge, Larchford, Milford, Palmer, Pocohontas, Pomeroy, Remsen	4	3	5	5	2	5
4 sch., Sioux City, Carroll, Early	1	2	1		1	3
	12	18	10	13	9	18

Summary:
  Dioceses approving DM, **7**
    24 churches
    16 colleges, schools

PROVINCE OF LOS ANGELES:

	Sdys only	Wkdys only	Sdys & Wkdys	Engl. only	Latin only	Engl.-Latin
44. *Los Angeles:* 2 ch., Alhambra, San Pedro 6 coll., sch., Los Angeles, Santa Barbara	I	I 6		2 I	 2	 3

45. *Monterey-Fresno:*

"There is no parish or church in this Diocese where the custom of Dialog Mass has been introduced. The Bishop has no regulations of his own concerning it and pastors have his full permission in such matters to proceed in accord with their own judgment of local conditions and that of the Holy See for the liturgical aspect.

"The movement is known to various pastors and communities of teaching nuns, but so far as our information goes only one parish contemplates the introduction of the method in the near future." — J. CULLETSON, *Chancellor-Secretary.*

46. *San Diego:*

"His Excellency does not think that the Dialog Mass would be practical as yet for this Diocese, as he has but recently introduced the use of the daily and Sunday Mass missal. In the future, however, when other more pressing matters are taken care of, we should be happy to have the opportunity to introduce the Dialog Mass in this Diocese." — KENNETH G. STACK, *Secretary.*

	Sdys only	Wkdys only	Sdys & Wkdys	Engl. only	Latin only	Engl.-Latin
47. *Tucson:* sch., Tucson		1			1	
	1	8		3	3	3

Summary:
Dioceses approving DM, 4
   2 churches,
   7 colleges, schools

PROVINCE OF LOUISVILLE:

	Sdys only	Wkdys only	Sdys & Wkdys	Engl. only	Latin only	Engl.-Latin
48. *Louisville:* 4 ch., Louisville 2 coll., Louisville, Nazareth	1	1	2 2		 2	4
49. *Covington:* ch., Southgate	1				1	
50. *Nashville:* No information at hand						
51. *Owensboro:* No information at hand						
	2	1	4		3	4

Summary:
Dioceses using DM, 2
   4 churches
   3 colleges, schools

PROVINCE OF MILWAUKEE:

	Sdys only	Wkdys only	Sdys & Wkdys	Engl. only	Latin only	Engl.-Latin
52. *Milwaukee:* 3 ch., Milwaukee, Sheboygan, West Allis 4 coll., sch., Milwaukee, Fond du Lac, Madison	1 1	2 3		2	 2	1 2
53. *Green Bay:* 2 ch., Kaukauna, Marinette		2		1		1

54. *La Crosse :*

"This excellent practice has been developing here for several years and is a natural, spontaneous growth. It has received commendation and encouragement on appropriate occasions from both my esteemed Auxiliary, Most Reverend William R. Griffin, and myself." — A. J. McGavick, *Bishop of La Crosse.*

	Sdys only	Wkdys only	Sdys & Wkdys	Engl. only	Latin only	Engl.-Latin
Cath., 10 ch., La Crosse, Chippewa Falls, Durand, Ellworth, Menomonie, Norwalk, Potosi, Sauk City, Wisconsin Rapids[7]	1	5	6	5	3	4
9 coll., sch., La Crosse, Auburndale, Chippewa Falls, Lima, Prairie du Chien, Sinsinawa, Wassau	1	3	5	2	3	4
55. *Superior:* Cath., ch., Rice Lake	1	1		1		1
	5	16	12	11	8	14

Summary:
   Dioceses using DM, 4
      19 churches
      14 colleges, schools

   [7] These sodalists' returns are to be compared with official survey, 86 churches, as set out in the following chapter.

PROVINCE OF NEWARK :

	Sdys only	Wkdys only	Sdys & Wkdys	Engl. only	Latin only	Engl.-Latin
56. *Newark:* Dialog Mass not permitted						
57. *Camden:* ch., Penn's Grove	1					1

58. *Paterson:*

"I wish to advise that I know of no place in the Diocese of Paterson where the Dialog Mass is being conducted. I would state also that we are not giving permission for the same. It appears to me that, while a greater participation of the laity is desirable at Mass, the Dialog Mass does not appear as a genuine contribution to the liturgical development since it leads the people away more and more from High Mass, which is the one which the faithful should participate in." — THOMAS H. McLAUGHLIN, *Bishop of Paterson.*

	Sdys only	Wkdys only	Sdys & Wkdys	Engl. only	Latin only	Engl.-Latin
59. *Trenton:* 2 ch., Long Branch, South Amboy	1		1	2		1
	2		1	2		1

Summary:
  Dioceses using DM, 2
    3 churches

PROVINCE OF NEW ORLEANS:

60. *New Orleans:*

"His Excellency Archbishop Rummel has requested me to inform you that he is not convinced that this method is uniformly desirable in the Archdiocese, but he leaves it to the individual priests to adopt it on trial.

"Dialog Mass was introduced at St. Catherine of Siena Church, Metairie,[8] a few years ago by the pastor, Father Leo Jarysch, and it is still kept up there. When Father Jarysch was transferred to St. Joseph's Church in Gretna,[8] he introduced Dialog Mass there.

[8] Not mentioned in sodality survey.

Our impression is that this method of assisting at holy Mass has been acceptable in both of these parishes. Personally I feel that the Dialog Mass, or *Missa Recitata,* will become more widespread with the growth of the liturgical movement through such media as the Liturgical Week, which I had the pleasure of attending in Chicago last October. It is certainly a laudable objective to strive after. — Sincerely yours in Christ," A. CARROLL BADEAUX, *Chancellor.*

	Sdys only	Wkdys only	Sdys & Wkdys	Engl. only	Latin only	Engl.-Latin
5 ch., New Orleans, Donaldsonville	I	I	3	4		I
5 coll., sch., New Orleans, Donaldsonville		4	I	2		2
61. *Alexandria:* Cath., ch., Alexandria		I	I	I	I	
3 coll., sch., Natchitoches, Shreveport		3		2	I	
62. *Lafayette:* Cath., Lafayette, ch., Iota	I	I				2
2 sch., Lafayette, Iota		2				2
63. *Little Rock:* 2 ch., Subiaco, Texarkana		I	I	2		

64. *Mobile:*

Survey afforded no information, but the Bishop's letter follows : "There are many churches in the Diocese that are using the *Missa Recitata,* but I have made no statement in regard to it. Wherever they asked me if they might use it, I have encouraged them, but have not urged it upon them. I could not say just how many parishes are making use of the *Missa Recitata.*" — T. J. TOOLEN, *Bishop of Mobile.*

	Sdys only	Wkdys only	Sdys & Wkdys	Engl. only	Latin only	Engl.-Latin
65. *Natchez:* 2 ch., Chatawa, Meridian	1		1	1		1
	3	13	8	12	2	10

Summary:
  Dioceses using DM, 6
    13 churches
    11 colleges, schools

PROVINCE OF NEW YORK:

	Sdys only	Wkdys only	Sdys & Wkdys	Engl. only	Latin only	Engl.-Latin
66. *New York:* 3 ch., New York, Dongan Hills 5 coll., sch., New York, New Rochelle	3 5			1	 2	2 3
67. *Albany:* ch., Rensselaer 5 coll., sch., Albany, Schenectady, Troy	1 4		 1	1	 1	 4
68. *Brooklyn:* 3 ch., Brooklyn coll., Brooklyn	2	1 1		2		1 1

69. *Buffalo:*

"Our priests are authorized to organize the Dialog Mass when they are sure it will be done correctly, that is, with the uniform and regular pronunciation of the Latin words, and with careful attention to the priest, so as not to delay him." — J. A. DUFFY, *Bishop of Buffalo.*
[1937]

	Sdys only	Wkdys only	Sdys & Wkdys	Engl. only	Latin only	Engl.-Latin
ch., Albion	1			1		
6 coll., sch., Buffalo, Eggertsville, Kenmore, Stella Niagara		4	1	2	2	2
70. *Ogdensburg:* No information at hand						
71. *Rochester:* ch., Webster	1				1	
sch., Rochester		1				1
72. *Syracuse:* 2 ch., Rome, Solvay	2			2		
sch., Syracuse	1					1
	11	18	1	9	6	15

Summary:
  Dioceses using DM, 6
    11 churches
    19 colleges, schools

PROVINCE OF PHILADELPHIA:

	Sdys only	Wkdys only	Sdys & Wkdys	Engl. only	Latin only	Engl.-Latin
73. *Philadelphia:* 3 coll., sch., Philadelphia, Bernharts	1		2		2	1

74. *Altoona:*

"I know Bishop Guilfoyle is interested in greater participation by the faithful in the Holy Sacrifice of the Mass. Since January 3, 1941, we have had the Dialog Mass in the Cathedral Convent here. . . . Bishop has had occasion to say Mass there several times and hence has experienced the conduct of the Dialog Mass. He speaks of it very favorably and would like to see it introduced in other places. . . . We intend to push the Dialog Mass gradually from this office and in our trips around the Diocese." — JOSEPH D. O'LEARY, *Vice-Chancellor.*

	Sdys only	Wkdys only	Sdys & Wkdys	Engl. only	Latin only	Engl.-Latin
5 ch., Altoona, Johnstown, Spangler, Windber	2	2	1		1	3
75. *Erie:* ch., Warren	1					1
coll., Erie		1				1
76. *Harrisburg:* 2 sch., Donville, Lancaster		2			1	1
77. *Pittsburgh:* 2 ch., Connellsville, McKeesport	2					2
4 sch., Pittsburgh, North Pittsburgh	2	2		1	3	
78. *Scranton:* sch., Williamsport		1		1		
	7	8	1	2	5	8

Summary:
Dioceses using DM, 6
  8 churches
  11 colleges, schools

PROVINCE OF PORTLAND:

79. *Portland:*

"In two churches of this Archdiocese, to my knowledge, the *Missa Recitata* is used, at least once each week, St. Francis of Assisi and St. Thomas More.

"You will also be interested in knowing, no doubt, that in both of these parishes the Ordinary of the Mass is sung on a great many Sundays by the entire congregation at High Mass." — EDWARD D. HOWARD, *Archbishop of Portland in Oregon.*

	Sdys only	Wkdys only	Sdys & Wkdys	Engl. only	Latin only	Engl.-Latin
2 ch., Portland		1	1	1		1
2 sch., Portland, St. Benedict	1		1		1	1
80. *Baker City:* No information at hand						
81. *Boise:* No information at hand						

82. *Great Falls:*

Sodalists' survey afforded no information : letter of Bishop's secretary follows :

"According to our information the Dialog Mass has been used in at least one parish of the Diocese, St. Mary's School of St. Ann's Cathedral.

"During the coming school year, His Excellency has suggested that the Dialog Mass be made a project

	Sdys only	Wkdys only	Sdys & Wkdys	Engl. only	Latin only	Engl.-Latin
Cath., Great Falls	1					
83. *Helena:* sch., Bozeman		1			1	
84. *Seattle:* 4 ch., Seattle, Cowlity Prairie, Vancouver	3	1		2	1	1
3 sch., Seattle, Cowlity Prairie, Tacoma		3		1	1	1
85. *Spokane:* ch., Walla Walla			1	1		
4 sch., Spokane, Sprague		2	2		1	3
	4	8	5	5	5	7

Summary:
 Dioceses using DM, 6
  8 churches
  10 schools

of the Great Falls Council of Catholic Youth. In our youth program for the coming year the Dialog Mass will definitely have a prominent place." — E. B. SCHUSTER, *Secretary to Bishop of Great Falls.*

86. *Alaska, Vic. Apos.:*

Sodality survey afforded no information : letter of Coadjutor Vicar :

"In the extensive districts of the Vicariate, Father Martin Lonneux, S.J., among others, has trained the Eskimos in the Dialog Mass. The whole congregation answered the prayers with the server, and as the missionary had supplied translations of the beautiful prayers, all these simple people understood and took part in the sublime Sacrifice of the Mass. I think that this method is the best means for the people properly to assist at low Mass. God bless the efforts to increase this practice so edifyingly portrayed among the illiterate but truly fervent and faithful Eskimos of the Northland." — WALTER J. FITZGERALD, S. J., *Coad. Vic. Apos. of Alaska.*

PROVINCE OF ST. LOUIS :

	Sdys only	Wkdys only	Sdys & Wkdys	Engl. only	Latin only	Engl.-Latin
87. *St. Louis:* 10 ch., St. Louis, Arcadia, Jefferson City, Martinsburg, Richmond Heights, St. Charles	2	3	5	3	1	6
13 sch., St. Louis, Arcadia, Clayton, Kirkwood, Webster Groves		9	4		4	9
88. *Concordia:* 2 ch., Collyer, Geoville		2		2		
coll., Hays		1				1

89. *Kansas City:*

"Since the 'dialogue' Mass is recognized as perhaps the most practical method of introducing popular participation in the liturgy of the Church, so ardently recommended by Pope Pius X and his successors in the Supreme Pontificate, we should look forward to encouraging it among the youth of all our parishes — and, in due time, to have our parish Mass on Sunday conducted in this manner.   There is no thought of being hurried in this matter, for haste would probably result in defeating any hope of permanent achievement.

"We are, however, desirous of making a beginning in connection with our diocesan Eucharistic Congress, a feature of which will be the exemplification of how to conduct a 'dialogue' Mass by the junior CYO groups of the diocese.   In preparation for this demonstration I am asking the pastors to have their junior CYO groups become acquainted with the Community Mass during April." — EDWIN V. O'HARA, *Bishop of Kansas City."*

90. *Leavenworth :*

"One of the most promising indications that we shall eventually achieve the full restoration of active lay participation in the sacred Mysteries, which is so ardently desired by the Holy See, is the rise and spread in recent years of the practice known as Dialog Mass.   We welcome it to the Diocese of Leavenworth.   We are heartily in favor of its use in religious houses and for the week-day Masses of children attending Catholic schools.   We are in favor of its introduction into the parishes, when the reverend pastors find that the ground has been sufficiently prepared, so that it can be done intelligently, reverently, smoothly.—Sincerely yours in Christ," PAUL C. SCHULTE, *Bishop of Leavenworth.*

	Sdys only	Wkdys only	Sdys & Wkdys	Engl. only	Latin only	Engl.-Latin
ch., Flush			1			1
6 sch., Leavenworth, Atchison, Blaine, St. Marys		3	3		4	2
3 coll., sch., Kansas City		2			2	1

	Sdys only	Wkdys only	Sdys & Wkdys	Engl. only	Latin only	Engl.-Latin
91. *St. Joseph:* Sodalists' survey afforded no information; others report: cath., St. Joseph; ch., Conception		1	1			
3 sch., Chillicothe, Conception, Marysville		2	1			

92. *Wichita:*

"We are not only in sympathy with this movement, but we are encouraging and introducing the Dialogue Mass wherever we can. I am confident that the time is most apropos to have the people come closer to the august Sacrifice and the liturgy of the Church, and to bring the liturgy to the people. I am convinced that much of this work will have to be done by our devoted religious. I am, therefore, most anxious to see the Dialogue Mass used every day in our convents, and, if possible, also the Offertory procession. The novices and the young sisters, who are preparing for their future work, will in consequence go to the missions enthusiastic for the proper participation of the laity in the Sacred Mysteries.

"In the first place, my own chapel, where my chauffeur and my two sisters join me in the active participation and in Offertory procession; the Cathedral, other churches, mother-houses, hospitals, convents, academies, . . .

"We deeply appreciate sustained interest in this most timely movement." — C. H. WINKELMANN, *Bishop of Wichita.*

	Sdys only	Wkdys only	Sdys & Wkdys	Engl. only	Latin only	Engl.-Latin
Bishop's chapel, Cathedral 10 ch., Wichita, Andale, Bison, Dodge City, Galena, Humboldt, Hutchinson, Independence, Odin, Pittsburg, Pratt, Windhorst	2	4	6	2	2	8
8 coll., sch., Wichita, Derby, Dodge City, Great Bend, Pittsburg		3	5		2	6
	4	31	26	7	15	34

Summary:
  Dioceses using DM, 6
  27 churches
  34 colleges, schools

PROVINCE OF ST. PAUL:

	Sdys only	Wkdys only	Sdys & Wkdys	Engl. only	Latin only	Engl.-Latin
93. *St. Paul:* 7 ch., St. Paul, Bud Island, Farmington, Minneapolis, Montgomery	2	1	4	2	3	2
2 sch., Faribault, Montgomery		1	1		2	
94. *Bismarck:* ch., Richardson		1		1		
sch., Bismark		1			1	

95. *Crookston:*

"I am much interested in the Dialog Mass and favor its introduction or use. All the parishes of the diocese that have parochial schools are using the Dialog Mass and even some of the other pastors have adopted it or at least attempted to introduce it. But I am somewhat disturbed by the evident lack of unity among the promoters as to what is correct, or what is even permissible and what is not. If your proposed work will serve to bring about a fuller understanding, it will have much to commend it.—Sincerely yours in Christ," J. H. Peschges, *Bishop of Crookston.*

	Sdys only	Wkdys only	Sdys & Wkdys	Engl. only	Latin only	Engl.-Latin
2 ch., Birmidge, Thief River sch., Crookston		I I	I		I	2
96. *Duluth:* coll., Duluth		I				I

97. *Fargo:*

"Observation with regard to the practical use of the Dialog Mass has led me to the conclusion that it should be restricted to small groups of persons who have learned to appreciate the Mass and who are able to use the missal properly.

"Otherwise the Dialog Mass should be used with discretion. I have found that with regard to children it leads to a great deal of confusion and inattention. I have observed that in the interval between the responses children are restless and inattentive; they do not say any other prayers whatsoever; if they are caught unawares when a response is to be made only a few make it. It is to be feared that the Dialog Mass used in general practice will lead to externalism with regard to personal devotion and liturgical worship.

"I should recommend the Dialog Mass be used for priests at their retreat or other gatherings whenever they assist at a low Mass; for nuns and sisters in convents, at least on certain occasions; as well as for small groups of our educated laity. I do not recommend the Dialog Mass for general congregational use." — A. J. MUENCH, *Bishop of Fargo.*

	Sdys only	Wkdys only	Sdys & Wkdys	Engl. only	Latin only	Engl.-Latin
ch., Devil's Lake	1				1	
2 sch., Devil's Lake, Grand Forks	1	1			2	
98. *Rapid City:* Cath., Rapid City; ch., Pine Ridge	1		1	1		1
2 sch., Pine Ridge, St. Francis		2			1	1
99. *St. Cloud:* Cath., St. Cloud, 2 ch., St. Joseph, Ward Springs			3		1	2
3 coll., sch., St. Cloud, Onamia, St. Joseph		2	1		2	1

100. *Sioux Falls:*

"In the Diocese of Sioux Falls the *Missa Recitata* or the Dialog Mass is celebrated not only with the approval but with the recommendation of the Ordinary. It is held daily in many of the convent and hospital chapels; wherever possible it is part of the school program. To insure proper introduction, the Ordinary has urged that it be introduced at first only among the groups trained for the purpose — the nuns, children, in school, etc. From this beginning, it is expected, as the children leave school and mingle with the adult congregation, to have a nucleus of trained and instructed persons who will be able to act as leaders and around whom the other adults can rally in taking their part. Here we have used the more expanded form, the group reciting not merely the answers of the Mass

	Sdys only	Wkdys only	Sdys & Wkdys	Engl. only	Latin only	Engl.-Latin
3 ch., Dell Rapids, Howard, Montrose 3 sch., Sioux Falls, Mitchell, Yankton	1	1 3	1			3 3
101. *Winona:* ch., Hokah sch., Lake City		1	1	1		1
	6	17	13	5	15	16

Summary:
  Dioceses using DM, 9
    20 churches
    16 colleges, schools

PROVINCE OF SAN ANTONIO:

	Sdys only	Wkdys only	Sdys & Wkdys	Engl. only	Latin only	Engl.-Latin
102. *San Antonio:* 5 ch., San Antonio, Helletsville, Yoakum 3 coll., sch., San Antonio		2 3	3	3		2 3
103. *Amarillo:* No information at hand						
104. *Corpus Christi:* No information at hand						
105. *Dallas:* 2 ch., Dennison, Marshall 2 sch., Dennison, Marshall	2	1	1	1 1		1 1
106. *Galveston:* ch., Galveston		1		1		

servers, but also the *Gloria, Credo, Sanctus* and *Bene-dictus,* the *Agnus Dei,* the *Confiteor* and triple *Dom-ine non sum dignus* before the people's Communion. Wherever used, after proper introduction, it has stimulated interest in the liturgical life of the Church and given a new meaning to the Divine Sacrifice." — WILLIAM O. BRADY, *Bishop of Sioux Falls.*

107. *Oklahoma City-Tulsa:*

"The Dialog Mass has been tried in this Diocese; tried a little but discussed much. It has given a good account of itself. I wish that it might be allowed opportunities oftener to do the same, for it brings realization of the eternal greatness of the Holy Sacrifice to the people who assist at it. The Dialog Mass unites faithful and priest in the most sublime act of worship of all time. If 'it is the Mass that matters' — and it is — what better could be done than to make the Mass matter more and more to the faithful by giving them a more intimate knowledge of every part of it?" — FRANCIS C. KELLEY, *Bishop of Oklahoma City and Tulsa.*

	Sdys only	Wkdys only	Sdys & Wkdys	Engl. only	Latin only	Engl.-Latin
4 ch., Oklahoma City, Enid, McAlester, Muskogee	1	2	1		1	3
4 coll., sch., Oklahoma City, El Reno, Enid, Tulsa	1	2	1	1	1	2
	4	11	6	7	2	12

Summary:
  Dioceses using DM, 4
    18 churches
    9 colleges, schools

PROVINCE OF SAN FRANCISCO:

	Sdys only	Wkdys only	Sdys & Wkdys	Engl. only	Latin only	Engl.-Latin
108. *San Francisco:* 2 ch., San Francisco sch, San Francisco	I	I I		2 I		
109. *Reno:* No information at hand						
110. *Sacramento:* Cath., Sacramento	I			I		
111. *Salt Lake City:* sch., Salt Lake		I			I	
	2	3		4	I	

Summary:
Dioceses using DM, 3
   3 churches
   2 schools

PROVINCE OF SANTA FE:

112. *Santa Fe:*

"Archbishop Gerken of Santa Fe told me they would start *Missa Recitata* in St. Michael's College, Santa Fe, and in the Lourdes Trades School at Aubuquerque." —Letter of BISHOP J. H. SCHLARMAN.

	Sdys only	Wkdys only	Sdys & Wkdys	Engl. only	Latin only	Engl.-Latin
2 ch., Las Vegas, Roswell 2 sch., Albuquerque, Las Vegas		2 2		I	I	I I
113. *El Paso:* ch., Carlsbad		I		I		
114. *Gallup:* sch., Prescott		I			I	
		6		2	2	2

Summary:
Dioceses using DM, 3
   3 churches
   3 schools

ADDITIONAL NOTE

Colleges Reporting Use of Dialog Mass, Sodality Survey

This list of colleges is by no means a complete roster of those using Dialog Mass, but merely records those so reporting in the Sodality Survey dealt with in the foregoing pages:

Barat College, Lake Forest, Ill.

Boston College, Boston, Mass.

Canisius College, Buffalo, N. Y.

Chaminade College, Clayton, Mo.

Clarke College, Dubuque, Ia.

College of St. Benedict, St. Joseph, Minn.

College of St. Rose, Albany, N. Y.

College of St. Scholastica, Duluth, Minn.

Creighton University, Omaha, Nebr.

Crosier College, Onamia, Minn.

Dominican College, New Orleans, La.

Edgewood Jr. College, Madison, Wis.

Fontbonne College, St. Louis, Mo.

Fordham University, New York, N. Y.

Georgetown University, Wash'n, D. C.

Incarnate Word College, San Antonio, Tex.

Loras College, Dubuque, Ia.

Loyola University, Los Angeles, Cal.

Loyola University, New Orleans, La.

Marian College, Indianapolis, Ind.

Marquette University, Milwaukee, Wis.

Marygrove College, Detroit, Mich.

Maryhurst College, Erie, N. Y.

Mary Manse College, Toledo, Ohio.

Monte Cassino College, Tulsa, Okla.

Mt. Marty Jr. College, Yankton, S. D.

Mt. Mary Jr. College, Cedar Rapids, La.

Mt. St. Agnes Jr. College, Mt. Washington, Md.

Mt. St. Scholastica College, Atchison, Kans.

Nazareth College, Nazareth, Ky.

New Rochelle College, New Rochelle, N. Y.

Notre Dame College, Baltimore, Md.

Notre Dame College, S. Euclid, Ohio.

Our Lady of the Elms College, Chicopee, Mass.

Our Lady of the Lake College, San Antonio, Tex.

Regis College, Weston, Mass.

Rockhurst College, Kansas City, Mo.

Rosemont College, Philadelphia, Pa.

Sacred Heart Jr. College, Wichita, Kans.

St. Catherine Jr. College, Louisville, Ky.

St. Francis College, Brooklyn, N. Y.

St. Francis College, Joliet, Ill.

St. Joseph's College, Hays, Kans.

St. Mary's College, Holy Cross, Ind.

St. Mary's College, Leavenworth, Kans.

St. Mary's of the Woods College, Ind.

St. Michael's College, Winooski Pk., Vt.

St. Procopius College, Lisle, Ill.

St. Teresa's College, Kansas City, Mo.

St. Vincent's College, Shreveport, La.

Trinity College, Washington, D. C.

Trinity College, Sioux City, Iowa.

University of Detroit, Detroit, Mich.

Webster College, Webster Groves, Mo.

Xavier University, Cincinnati, Ohio.

GENERAL SUMMARY, SODALISTS' USE OF DIALOG MASS

Province	Dioceses approv. DM.	Dioceses not approv. DM.	D. no inform.	Churches	Schools	Sundays only	Wkdys only	Sdys & Wkdys	English only	Latin only	Engl.-Latin
Baltimore	6		3	10	15	5	16	3	6	4	12
Boston	7	1		13	13	8	9	7	5	8	7
Chicago	4	1		15	31	8	32	5	3	17	25
Cincinnati	6			13	26	4	26	7	7	12	18
Denver	3			3	2	1	3	1	2	2	1
Detroit	5			22	6	5	7	16	5	8	15
Dubuque	7			24	16	12	18	10	13	9	18
Los Angeles	4			2	7	1	8		3	3	3
Louisville	2		2	4	3	2	1	4		3	4
Milwaukee	4			19	14	5	16	12	11	8	14
Newark	2	2		3		2		1	2		1
New Orleans	6			13	11	3	13	8	12	2	10
New York	6		1	11	19	11	18	1	9	6	15
Philadelphia	6			8	11	7	8	1	2	5	8
Portland (Ore.)	6		2	8	10	4	8	5	5	5	7
St. Louis	6			27	34	4	31	26	7	15	34
St. Paul	9			20	16	6	17	13	5	15	16
San Antonio	4		2	12	9	4	11	6	7	2	12
San Francisco	3		1	3	2	2	3		4	1	
Santa Fe	3			3	3		6		2	2	2
TOTALS	99[1]	4	11	233	248	95	251	126	110	127	222
						20%	52%	28%	25%	27%	48%

[1] Honolulu makes the hundredth see.

CHAPTER VII

LA CROSSE POINTS THE WAY

One is forcibly reminded that *La Crosse* is the
French for *crozier,* that pastoral staff, emblem of the
bishop's duty "to conciliate the minds of hearers
whilst fostering virtues," as the *Pontificale* puts it.
The bishop's crozier points the way for the Diocese of
La Crosse in the matter of the Dialog Mass.

In tabulating the returns of the sodalists' survey
dealt with in the previous chapter, the writer was
struck by unusually heavy returns for the La Crosse
diocese. Eleven churches in widely-scattered parts of
the area, and no less than nine academies, high schools,
schools of nursing, conducted by several different religious congregations, and representing both smaller
and larger population centers, reported on the use of
the Dialog Mass by their sodalists. These numbers,
while not large, are out of all proportion to most other
dioceses of equal size. Again, in the matter of frequency, the returns read daily, daily, daily, five days
a week, four days, and so forth, indicating that the
Dialog Mass is firmly and deeply rooted. Lastly, in
arrangement the Dialog Mass as used was in many instances discovered to be complex and comprehensive,
and in some cases the absolute limit for the scope of
active lay participation was recorded as of daily usage.
The reports, from every angle, indicated that La Crosse
in the matter of the Dialog Mass was decidedly different. There are aspects of democracy and the good

life that we have been taught to associate with Wisconsin progressiveness. Here it would seem that lands linked forever with names like Joliet and La Salle, Allouez and Marquette, were now furnishing progressive leadership in the spreading in America of what the Holy See is pleased to call "this praiseworthy form of liturgical piety." Why was La Crosse in this respect different?

That question raised a challenge, and the writer addressed it to the shepherd who carries the crozier, His Excellency Most Reverend Alexander J. McGavick, D.D. "Naturally," I stated, after explaining the survey among sodalists and its results, "it is of special interest to know why the Dialog Mass is making far greater strides in this diocese over so many others. To what initial impetus is this owing, would you say? To what combination of circumstances would you ascribe such a spread of this mode of Mass-assistance? What official direction has Your Excellency given in the matter?"

A few days later I received a gracious and modest reply:

"I would state that this excellent practice," the letter began, formalities over, "has been developing here for several years and is a natural, spontaneous growth. It has received commendation and encouragement on appropriate occasions from both my esteemed Auxiliary, Most Reverend William R. Griffin, and myself."

So, in first instance, however modestly glossed over, the crozier had pointed out the path. The shepherd went on to attribute the growth to the zeal of the clergy in combination with the Catholic Youth Organization:

"That encouragement does not wholly account for

Left: La Crosse Youth Congress Dialog Mass. *Upper Right:* Bishop Alter Celebrating Dialog Mass. *Lower Right:* Dialog Mass, St. Francis Xavier's College, Brooklyn.

the way the practice has spread, and I am convinced that the real explanation of the matter is found only in the fine spiritual basis of our flourishing Catholic Youth Organization and the piety and zeal of the reverend clergy.

"Our CYO, in the cultivation of the spiritual as its primary activity through the Sodality, has had a most favorable influence on our youth, making them spiritual minded, and arousing in them a measure of apostolic interest.

"In that disposition, I would say, lies the explanation of this leaning to a fuller participation in the Mass through the Dialog method, a disposition encouraged and made much of by the devotion of many of our priests."

His Excellency's letter added this question, which under the circumstances, came close to being tantalizing:

"May I finally state that your list of parishes, schools and institutions where the Dialog Mass is customary in our Diocese is to my personal knowledge far from complete?"

This was bait, and it shortly evoked the counter-query if I might be sent what positive information was at hand. My next communication from His Excellency was dated a week later. Meanwhile not a little had happened, as I saw to my amazement on reading:

"*April* 1, 1941.

"My dear Father Ellard: After receiving your letter of March 25th, Bishop Griffin sent out a card (copy enclosed) to all pastors asking for a report on the use of the Dialog Mass or *Missa Recitata*. He has so far received 83 replies with 50 of these reporting in the affirmative, 33 in the negative and 3 stating that they expect to start the Dialog Mass after Easter. Some stated that they used this method of hearing Mass on week-day mornings for children, even public school children. Bishop did not send cards to schools or institutions, as we know that all these use the Dialog Mass. We have 158 parishes and I believe that in at least one half of these the Dialog Mass is in regular use.

"Wishing you a joyous Easter, I am, . ."

The card was a postal card, addressed to Most Reverend Wm. R. Griffin, D.D., presenting this form:

Parish . . . .
City or town. . . . .
Do you have the *Missa Recitata* in your parish?

Yes ☐　　　　　　　　No ☐

How often do you have the *Missa Recitata?*

Every Sunday? ☐

How many Sundays a month? ☐

Every week day? ☐

How many days a week? ☐

Do children only take part? Yes ☐　　　No ☐

Do adults also take part? Yes ☐　　　No ☐

. . . .
Pastor

Not long thereafter the cards received up to April 26th were loaned me, and with them came a covering letter from Reverend Stephen Anderl, Executive Secretary of the Catholic Youth Organization. Further on we list the parishes, inserting a few known from the sodalists' list, and the reports they furnished. For the sake of quick comparison we indicate at the extreme right hand side whether or not the parish was previously reported through the sodality survey. After scanning the lists there will be an opportunity for comparisons, and observations, and aspirations!

"The encouragement of our bishops is, of course, the big reason for the common practice of the Dialog Mass," stated the Reverend Stephen Anderl, Executive Secretary of the Catholic Youth Organization when forwarding the data to the writer. He thus described the function and method of CYO in spreading this impulse throughout the Diocese at the present time:

"The CYO holds two large conventions annually, one in October called the Youth Congress, which is really a convention of the diocesan Parish Sodality Union, and one in May, the diocesan High School Sodality Union Convention. The former is attended by more than 3000 young people and the latter by about 1000. Each of these conventions always opens with a pontifical low Mass as *Missa Recitata*. In spite of the fact that the group is very large, and that they are from many different parishes and schools, we have no trouble in conducting it at all, perhaps because most of those present are so familiar with the practice from their own parishes. The Masses at these meetings are attended by about 2000 and 600 to 700 respectively. I usually lead the *Missa Recitata* at the October meeting myself, and the method followed is that contained in the little booklet published by *The Queen's Work* entitled *Community Mass (Missa Recitata)*."

DIOCESE OF LA CROSSE, CHURCHES USING DIALOG MASS

Church	Pastor	Sndys, how often?	Wkdys, how many?	Children only?	For Adults also?	Reported, Sodality survey?
La Crosse,						
St. Joseph's Cath'l	Msgr. P. Pape	Wkly	4	Yes		Yes
Holy Cross	Msgr. S. Andrzejewski	Wkly	2	Yes		
Holy Trinity	V. Rev. C. W. Gille	Mthly	1	Yes	Yes	Yes
St. James	L. B. Keegan	Mthly	6	No	Yes	Yes
St. John Baptist	J. Pitz	Mthly	6	No		
St. Mary	Msgr. R. B. Condon	Mthly	4			
St. Wenceslaus	Msgr. F. Cech	Mthly	2	No	Yes	
Bl. Sacrament	V. J. Plecity	Occ'ly	1			
Adams, St. Joseph	J. L. Brudermanns	Wkly	Lent	Yes		
Alma, St. Lawrence	L. Scheuring	Biwkly	Vac. Sch	Yes		
Altoona, St. Mary	J. Schulte, O.M.I.		5	Yes		
Athens, St. Anthony	N. W. Thomas		3	Yes		
Auburndale, St. Mary	J. Steinhauser		1	Yes		
Bakerville, Corpus Christi	A. J. Cramer		3	Yes		
Baraboo, St. Joseph	Msgr. E. C. O'Reilly	Mthly	3	Yes		
Big River Falls, St. Joseph	V. Peters			No		
Big River, St. Mary	E. L. Knauf		5	Yes	Yes	
Blanchardville, Immaculate Conception	B. Duffy	Wkly	5	No		
Blenker, St. Kilian	L. E. Stieber		4	Yes	Yes	
Bloomer, St. Paul	A. Frisch	Wkly	6	No	Yes	
Bloomington, St. Mary	W. M. Braun	Mthly	1	Yes	Yes	
Boscobel, Immaculate Conception	J. A. McNamara	Wkly	6	No	Yes	
Cadott, St. Rose	G. F. Schuh	Occ'ly	3	No	Yes	

Parish	Pastor	Instruction	Vac. Sch.			
Cashton, Sts. Peter & Paul	W. Daniels	Mthly	4	Yes	Yes	Yes
Cazenovia, St. Anthony	A. J. Daniels		4	Yes	Yes	Yes
Chippewa Falls						
Notre Dame	E. McGuigan, C.S.Sp.	Mthly	6	No	Yes	Yes
St. Charles B.	Msgr. J. L. Kaiser	Biwkly	3	No	Yes	
Clayfield, Lady Perp. Help.	R. J. Bindl		Yes		Yes	
Colby, St. Mary	L. J. Lang		2	Yes	No	
Cook's Valley, St. John Baptist	J. B. Everhardy	Starting	6	Yes	No	
Cuba City, St. Rose	L. Barney			Yes	Yes	
Darlington, Holy Rosary	V. Rev. B. Doyle	Mthly	5	No	No	
Dickeyville, Holy Ghost	C. W. Haines	Occ'ly	6	No	Yes	
Dorchester, St. Louis	P. H. Weller	Wkly	6	No	Yes	
Durand, Assumption	M. J. Kelnhofer	Mthly	1	Yes	Yes	Yes
Eastman, St. Wenceslaus	E. Bettinger	Vac. Sch.	Vac. Sch.		Yes	
Eau Claire						
St. Patrick	Msgr. C. Dowd	Biwkly	3	Yes		
Sacred Heart	F. X. Orthen	Mthly		Yes		
Eau Galle, St. Henry	N. E. King	Occ'ly	3	Yes		
Edgar, St. John Baptist	A. L. Oibert	Biwkly	5	No		
Elroy, St. Patrick	J. R. Murphy	Mthly				
Fairview, St. Joseph	J. J. Sheridan	Biwkly	1	Yes		
Galloway, St. Joseph	L. Slisz	Wkly	6	No		
Genoa, St. Charles	L. Seemann		5	Yes		
Greenwood, St. Mary	J. Novak	3	3	No		
Hewitt, St. Michael	J. Neises		3	No		
Hillsboro, St. Aloysius	C. J. Smetana		3	Yes		
Kendall, St. Joseph	W. T. Hackner	Biwkly	Vac. Sch.	No		

DIOCESE OF LA CROSSE, CHURCHES USING DIALOG MASS—*Continued*

Churches	Pastor	Sndys, How often?	Wkdys, How many?	Children only?	For Adults also?	Reported Sodality survey?
Lancaster, St. Clement	A. A. Hoffmann	Mthly	1	Yes	Yes	
Lima, Holy Rosary	J. Eisenmann		5	No	Yes	
Loyal, St. Anthony	A. Zinthefer		3	No	Yes	
Lyndon Station, St. Mary	L. P. Strofer	Mthly	2	No		
Marathon Nativity B.V.M.	E. A. Beyer	3	2	Yes		
Mauston, St. Patrick	G. Schleicher		2	Yes		
Menomonie, St. Joseph	J. F. Kundinger	Wkly	4	No	Yes	Yes
Middle Ridge, St. Peter	H. C. Koehler		3	Yes	Yes	
Neillsville, St. Mary	J. A. Biehler, C.PP.S.	Wkly	5	No	Yes	Yes
Norwalk, St. Augustine	E. W. Mechler	Mthly	4			
Pittsville, St. Joachim	J. Willitzer		1	No	Yes	
Platteville, St. Mary	F. X. Gray	Mthly	5	No	Yes	
Plum City, St. John B.	N. E. Kreibich		5	Yes		
Poniatowski, Holy Family	F. H. Kupka		2	Yes		
Potosi						
St. Thomas Apostle	J. Uduluth	Mthly	3	No	Yes	Yes
St. Andrew (Tennyson)	V. Rev. M. Haas		4	No	Yes	
Prairie du Chien, St. John Nepomuc.	P. J. Monarski		3			
Richland Center, St. Mary	O. Mitchell	Mthly	5	Yes	Yes	
Rozellville, St. Andrew	H. Lachnit		2	No		
Rudolph, St. Philemona	P. J. Wagner	Biwkly	4	Yes		
St. Joseph, St. Joseph	J. B. Pinion	Mthly	3	Yes		
St. Mary's Ridge, Nativity of B.V.M.	L. H. Timmerman	Mthly	3	Yes		

Parish	Pastor		Frequency			
Sauk City, St. Aloysius	F. Forster	4	Mthly	Yes		Yes
Sinsinawa, St. Joseph	H. J. Hoffmann	3	Starting	Yes		
Soldiers Grove, St. Philip	G. P. Mathieu	1	Wkly	No	Yes	
Sparta, St. Patrick	Msgr. H. F. Flock		Mthly			
Spencer, Christ King	J. Graf, C.PP.S.					
Spring Valley						
Sacred Heart	G. R. Hardy	6	Biwkly	No	Yes	
St. Joseph Mission	G. R. Hardy		Biwkly	No	Yes	
Stanley, St. Anne	P. Pitzenberger	2		Yes		
Tilden, St. Peter	R. F. Raschke	3		Yes		
Tomah, St. Mary	J. Brudermanns	3		Yes		
Waumandee, St. Boniface	A. W. Fischer	2	Occ'ly	No	Yes	Yes
Wausau, St. Mary	Msgr. J. B. Hauck	6		Yes		
Wilton, St. John	W. Baer	2	Wkly	Yes	Yes	
Wisconsin Rapids, Sts. Peter & Paul	Msgr. W. Reding	6		No	Yes	
Wonewoc, St. Jerome	A. J. Thuecks		Mthly	No		
Wuerzburg, St. John B.	F. Brickl					

Churches certainly using Dialog Mass, 86 or 54%.
Total of these churches using it Sundays and weekdays, 44 or 51%.
Total reporting adult participation, 34.
Total reporting youth participation, 43.

How this movement was first set on foot in the CYO itself, and through it into the parishes, is justly deemed by Father Anderl "an interesting sidelight on the survey, and a partial explanation for the somewhat uniform manner in which it is conducted." This is the story:

"The first time the *Missa Recitata* was used at the October Youth Congress, in order to encourage the spread of this practice among as many as possible of the parishes of the Diocese, the following was done: We selected a small group of young people from a particular parish (about 75), who had never gone to a parochial school, and who were offering Mass regularly in this fashion (they were not especially trained for the occasion), made certain they were conducting it correctly, and then in the presence of the large assembly at the pontifical low Mass carried on the Dialog Mass. In his sermon at that Mass and in his talks during the convention Bishop Griffin encouraged the practice of the *Missa Recitata,* pointing out that if this group of public school students could do the thing so well, it surely could be made a common practice among all youth groups and parishes in the Diocese. The following year at the October meeting the entire assembly took part in the *Missa Recitata* and have done so ever since."

The results can well speak for themselves. In a diocese very predominantly rural, where senior and junior central and parochial high schools number no more than twenty, at least 86 churches (54%) are using Dialog Mass. Of these 86 churches, 44 (51%) now use it on both Sundays and weekdays. The returns on the relative participation by youth and adult groups are both instructive and encouraging: 34 churches report adult participation along with the young people, while 43 have thus far communal participation by the young people only.   What began as a feature of the high school and post-school groups some years ago has now won footing in more than half the churches of the region, and is now shared in by adults in three churches to every four where the youth alone take their part in it.   The Ordinary and Auxiliary commend and encourage this practice, and praise the zeal of the priests and the young people.   The priest closest to the CYO says that the encouragement of the bishops is, of course, the dominating factor in this spread of the Dialog Mass.

There is still another powerful factor, mentioned with praise by both bishop and priest, and this is the contribution of the Sisters.   "We know that all these [Sisters' institutions] use the Dialog Mass," said Bishop McGavick, and Father Anderl's phrasing is: "The *Missa Recitata* is a common practice in these institutions. . . ."   In the sodalists' survey the secondary schools were a close second to the parishes, and even in the parishes the influence of the teaching Sisters must have often meant the difference between Dialog Mass and no Dialog Mass.

People are singularly sensitive to religious influence whilst patients in a hospital.   In the survey carried out by the sodalists, hospitals in La Crosse, Chippewa Falls, Marshfield and Wassau reported the Dialog Mass as a daily feature.   But what doubtless counts for more than any other influence exerted by the sisterhoods in this matter is the fact that such motherhouses as St. Rose's, La Crosse, and St. Clare's, Sinsinawa, set down Dialog Mass as of daily occurrence. The *Catholic Directory* discloses that parish after par-

ish reporting the use of Dialog Mass enjoys the services
of religious from these motherhouses. Here, I believe, one sees realized what Bishop Winkelmann is
striving for in Wichita. We have quoted the words
before, but they can well bear the repetition: "I am
most anxious," says His Excellency, "to see the Dialog
Mass used every day in our convents. . . . The novices and young religious, who are preparing for their
future work, will in consequence go to the missions
enthusiastic for the proper participation of the laity in
the Sacred Mysteries."

One final question imposes itself: Of what value is
this official survey in the La Crosse diocese for a true
estimate of the sodality inquiry, to which it here ran
parallel? The sodalists' survey reported eleven
churches in the diocese using Dialog Mass: the diocesan investigation brought this number up to eighty-
six, with many pastors still to be heard from. Eighty-
six is just short of being eight times the original eleven.
Could one, therefore, say that the sodalists' figures are
just a bare fraction of the true incidence of Dialog
Mass throughout the country? There is nothing in
the nature of a sodality monopoly in the use of the
Dialog Mass, and the writer knows of instances in
diocese after diocese where the current use of Dialog
Mass, having no relation to the sodality, is not covered
in the sodality survey. But making all such allow-
ances, it still would be very rash to try to arrive at an
estimate based on calculations supplied by comparing
the sodality figures for La Crosse diocese with the
much more ample and accurate data supplied by that
diocese itself.

The La Crosse diocese illustrates how the Dialog
Mass can in the course of some years be made to flour-

ish on a diocesan-wide basis by episcopal commendation and priestly zeal. But the Holy See leaves the adoption or non-adoption of the Dialog Mass entirely up to the bishop. If he adopts it, well and good; should he not see fit to do so, not the least shadow of discredit should be considered by that fact as reflecting on him. Our loyalty lies therein that we march behind our bishops' croziers. The shepherding of our souls is to them entrusted.

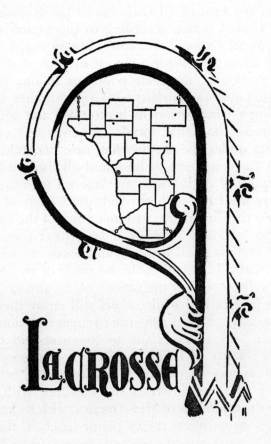

CHAPTER VIII

CHICAGOLAND'S OFFICIAL SURVEY

Seven per cent of all Catholics of the Roman Rite in the United States, according to the figures of the 1941 *Official Catholic Directory,* live in the Archdiocese of Chicago. Within the 3620 square miles of that jurisdiction, the most populous in our nation, something over 1900 priests serve 430 churches, as well as staffing a wide variety of institutions and agencies, educational, charitable, social. Among the 1,536,100 Catholics under the shepherding care of Archbishop Samuel A. Stritch are to be found all the conditions that make the Archdiocese an America in miniature. The city itself has its heavy industrial areas of mills, factories, packing-plants, with not a few of the foreign-language 'national' parishes of yesterday; then there are the endless small business and tenement sections, some already 'blighted' in the language of realtors because of the ceaseless migrations of an almost 'propertyless proletariat,' while others still enjoy their day of prosperity, or even affluence ; remoter sections and suburban fringes, especially to the west and north, afford a picture of living as care-free to the eye and opulent as any in the land. Chicagoland, with its amalgam of races, interests and cultures, with roots deep in the traditions of Mid-America, with its bustling 'busyness' as native as mince pie or baseball, this city

CHICAGOLAND'S OFFICIAL SURVEY 143

is a fair specimen of America-in-miniature. For that reason an authentic picture of the status of Dialog Mass in Chicagoland is a valuable bird's-eye view of what one may expect to find sooner or later in the nation itself.

Additional reasons suggesting Chicago's suitability for a Dialog Mass survey were these : For a decade or so the city has had an extremely energetic union of its sodalists of secondary-school age in Cisca (Chicago Interscholastic Catholic Action) , which, with the permission of the Chancery, has sponsored Dialog Mass widely. To the best of my knowledge there was never any direct support given to Cisca's efforts on behalf of Dialog Mass under the episcopacy of His Eminence, the late Cardinal Mundelein. Again, Cisca in 1939 itself made a partial survey of Dialog Mass, listing twenty-eight parishes in the city, four others in suburbs, then using Dialog Mass.[1] Too, since the coming of Archbishop Stritch to the city, there has been a very noticeable positive support to the entire program of the liturgical movement by the Ordinary, as was evidenced most clearly when His Excellency sponsored the first National Liturgical Week, October, 1940. Lastly, Liturgical Week itself, by bringing over twelve hundred people together in Chicago, should have afforded an enormous impetus to all previously existing tendencies in this direction. Thus, a Chicago survey at this time would serve to mark local advance over known conditions at definite dates in the past.

When the oft-mentioned sodality survey on Dialog Mass was in progress, it was pointed out to Archbishop Stritch that an *official* survey on the same subject might disclose valuable data, and so be of unques-

[1] Cf. *Orate Fratres*, XIV, 1 (Nov. 26, 1939), 19-25.

tioned advantage to the Ordinary.   To this His Excellency graciously replied :

"*March 24th,* 1941.

"My dear Father Ellard : I am much pleased that you are making a study on the Dialog Mass in our parishes and institutions.   Your findings will be very helpful to me.   I suggest that you get in touch with Monsignor Morrison and work out an interrogatory. We shall send it through our Chancery and have it returned to Monsignor Morrison, who will give you the findings for your study.   Sincerely yours in Christ, etc."

As the result of this letter an interrogatory for parishes was framed and one for institutions.   These were in time printed and distributed.   That for parishes is appended herewith, along with the covering letter of Rt. Rev. Monsignor George J. Casey, Chancellor.

"*May 6th,* 1941.

"Reverend and dear Father : We are making a survey of the present practice in all parishes of the archdiocese regarding the *Missa Recitata* or Dialog Mass, i.e., the recitation of certain parts of the Mass by the congregation.   You are asked to fill in the attached form and mail it to the Chancery Office.   Your prompt cooperation will be appreciated.

"With all good wishes, [etc.]."

QUESTIONNAIRE ON USE OF MISSA RECITATA IN PARISHES

1.   *Missa Recitata* is not in use in this church ☐

2.   *Missa Recitata* is in use in this church ☐ Since approximately ....
....

3.   *Missa Recitata* is used here on Sundays at Children's Mass ☐ How often ....

Chicago *New World*

S. A. STRITCH
Archbishop of Chicago

"We are getting the Dialog Mass to where it belongs"

4. *Missa Recitata* is used here on Sundays for adult congregations ☐

At how many Masses .... How often

....

5. *Missa Recitata* is used here on weekdays ☐ How often ....

....

6. In *Missa Recitata*, as used here, the leader reads parts of Proper ☐

7. In *Missa Recitata*, as used here, the leader does not read parts of Proper ☐

8. In *Missa Recitata*, as used here, is any part of Canon (*Te igitur* to *Pater Noster* exclusive) read aloud? ☐ State what part ....

....

9. In *Missa Recitata*, as used here, the parts checked are said in English or in Latin: (Where differing forms are in use Sundays and weekdays please indicate)

ENGLISH	LATIN
	☐ Altar-boy responses
☐ I Confess	☐ *Iudica — Confiteor*
☐ Lord have mercy (*Kyrie*)	☐ *Kyrie eleison*
☐ Glory to God	☐ *Gloria in excelsis*
☐ I believe	☐ *Credo*
☐ Offertory Prayers	
☐ Holy, holy, holy	☐ *Sanctus*
☐ Lamb of God	☐ *Agnus Dei*
☐ Lord Jesus Christ	☐
☐ I Confess	☐ *Confiteor*
☐ Lord, I am not worthy	☐ *Domine non sum dignus*

....

Pastor

....

Church

This chapter presents a partial digest of the returns of this Chicagoland survey. Incidentally, too, it provides optimistic comment, eight years after, on the following reflections voiced editorially in the Chicago *New World* in 1933: "It will require both time and patience, and the Church has an immense storehouse

of both, to bring back the people to the liturgy of the
Church. . . . In many places in Germany and in
Austria, the 'Recited Mass,' the outspoken participation in the Mass, is the ordinary way of assisting. All
of which gives proof that the universal priesthood of
believers, according to the text, 'you are a royal priesthood,' has actuality. Just in proportion as the laity
enters into participation of the liturgy will its beauty,
power and grace become known and reverenced." [2]
It will be seen from the following paragraphs that even
an eight-year draft on the Church's immense storehouse of time and patience has seen the silent church-
by-church penetration of Dialog Mass into *more than
one hundred parishes* (25%) and into some 65% of
the non-parochial schools and colleges. Another eight
or ten-year period will doubtless put the Dialog Mass
on a common footing in all religious houses and institutions, if not into that position thus described by the
Bishop of Kansas City: "We should look forward . . .
in due time to have our parish Mass on Sunday conducted in this manner."

Before listing the parishes where Dialog Mass is now
in use, we may note with interest the reasons alleged
by some pastors for *discontinuing* it, as well as those
advanced by others as to why it has not thus far been
introduced into their churches. "We had the Dialog
Mass *a couple of times,**" writes one pastor, "but it
did not seem to find favor with the people." Another
suburban pastor states without further explanation:
"The children had the practice up to last year."
Again, a Chicago pastor states (with a sigh?): "A few
years ago we introduced the Missal and attempted to

recite prayers aloud. It was discontinued." The reason for discontinuance was thus stated by another pastor : "*Missa Recitata* was used here for adults for the period of one year. It was discontinued because of the difficulty in meeting bus schedules." In one church it was discontinued partially on account of expense : "Some seven or eight years ago we introduced the *Missa Recitata* at the Children's Mass and the 10:00 and 11:00 o'clock Masses, but we found it an expensive affair. Ninety per-cent of the leaflets were unpaid for and we couldn't afford to keep it up." This pastor concludes with a special *NB* : "Would you believe it, but there are some people who tell us that the *reciting* of the Mass *aloud* serves only as a distraction for them !" This objection is more widespread than the pastor's amazement would lead him to suspect, and itself indicates the necessity of restoring popular participation in worship before the very idea of it withers away !

Comments of those pastors who do not use Dialog Mass might here be introduced by this testimony : "During the retreat last month (April) for our Commercial girls we had it three mornings, and it was impressive." Another pastor explains : "Because of the many different nationalities we have never started." "The custom here is to pray the Rosary each morning in low Masses." The writer feels grateful, with no disparagement of the Rosary intended, to record that only two pastors gave that explanation. "We have music at every Mass on Sundays," states a suburban pastor, while an urban *confrère* writes : "At the Children's Mass on weekdays, the children sing hymns in the vernacular during Mass." "We have eleven Masses on Sunday, and are pressed for time," wrote

another, and yet another : "Sunday's time is too short
for *Missa Recitata*."   Among the methods in use by
pastors for teaching the Mass, the introduction of the
missal is mentioned by one after another.   As a sample
of this type of answer, one might quote the following :
"We explain the Mass to the children by hearing the
Mass with them, using the Stedman Missal.   This plan
takes place every other Sunday, the other Sundays being given to the beginners."   In a diocese as large as
Chicago it is not surprising to find one pastor writing
across his questionnaire : "I have to admit that I did
not even know about the thing.   I do not know if it
is possible [here].   We used to have it in the old country."   His doubt as to its possibility here is probably
grounded on the problem of two or more spoken languages among the parishioners : several pastors mention the problem.   That and all the other difficulties
here advanced will be weighed objectively and discussed frankly farther on in this book.   Here let us
pass to the hundred-odd parishes reporting some use of
Dialog Mass.

When Father Stedman wrote of the Dialog Mass in
My Sunday Missal, "An edifying example of its success
is found in the Archdiocese of Chicago, where it inspires a larger and more devout attendance," he doubtless had in mind various news-items emanating from
the Midwest metropolis these last few years.   As a
priest he would have been impressed by the fact that
Dialog Mass is the daily order in the Philosophers'
Chapel, the Theologians' Chapel and the Deacons'
Chapel of St. Mary of the Lake Seminary; or, that the
Chicago Nocturnal Adoration Society monthly gathers
one thousand men into Notre Dame Church for worship that has its climax in Dialog Mass shortly after

midnight; or, that Reverend Hugh Calkins, O.S.M., known nationally as a promoter of the Novena of the Sorrowful Mother, is known in Chicago also as the founder of a popular Pray the Mass School for adults.

Or Father Stedman may have felt the force of Cisca (Chicago's Inter-Student Catholic Action), whose mammoth gatherings, inaugurated with Dialog Mass, are not only directly benefiting the young people themselves, but gradually preparing the scene for the use of this type of low Mass worship on a city-wide scope. It will not escape pastors the country over that the spread of Dialog Mass in Chicago, all the more impressive because of the absence of official encouragement, was due to the penetrating force of its sheer attractiveness.

In presenting these tables a few words of explanation are required. Most of the questionnaires returned were only partially filled in, and much of the information sought was not forthcoming : there are thus many blank spaces in the columns. The first column indicates whether or not the church now using Dialog Mass was so recorded in the Cisca survey of 1939; the second column registers such churches as were included in the sodality survey of this year. By "English only" we here mean that the questionnaires indicated the use by the group of the vernacular only, whether this was English, Polish, Lithuanian, Slovak or Italian, the altar-boy always answering in Latin.

Chicago Parishes Using Dialog Mass

Parish	Pastor	Cisca Survey 1939	Sod. Survey 1941	How long?	Sdy, Chd'n	Sdy, Adults	Wkly	Leader	Engl. only	Latin only	Engl.-Latin
1 Cathedral	Msgr. J. P. Morrison			Apr 1940	mthly	occ.	feasts	x		x	
2 St. Adelbert	Rev. C. I. Gronkowski			1912	wkly				Polish		
3 St. Adrian	Rev. L. McNamara	x			wkly					x	
4 St. Agnes	Msgr. I. Kestl		x	1931	mthly	One Mass wkly	freq				x[3]
5 St. Ailbe	Rev. E. V. Turner			Jan 1941	wkly			x			x
6 All Saints	Rev. D. Harnett				wkly						x
7 St. Aloysius	Rev. B. Laukemper	x		1934		2, 3 Masses wkly	freq	x			x
8 St. Alphonsus	Rev. F. Fagen, C. SS. R.				wkly				x		
9 St. Ambrose	Msgr. Wm. Foley	x			wkly				x		
10 St. Andrew	Rt. Rev. B. J. Sheil, D.D.	x	x			twice yrly					

11 St. Angela	Msgr. F. M. O'Brien	x	1938	wkly			x	x	x		
12 St. Benedict	Rev. W. Fasnacht			wkly				x	x	x	
13 St. Bernard	Msgr. J. F. Ryan					once wkly			x		
14 Bl. Sacrament	Rev. R. O'Brien			wkly				x	x		
15 St. Bonaventure	Rev. V. M. Moran	x		wkly	wkly		x	x	x		
16 St. Cajetan	Rev. G. Meade		Sept 1940		mthly		x	x			
17 St. Cath. Gen.	Rev. F. L. Byrnes		1937	wkly			x	x			
18 Corp. Christi	Rev. N. Christoffel, O.F.M.		Sept 1940			once wkly			x		
19 St. Edward	Rev. J. J. O'Hearn	x	1938	wkly			x		x		
20 St. Elizabeth	Rev. B. Drescher, S.V.D.		1939	wkly			x				x
21 St. Florian	Rev. F. A. Kulinski		Nov 1940	wkly	one Mass	x	x	x			
22 St. Francis Xavier	Rev. J. Liebreich	x		wkly	mthly	freq	x	x			
23 St. Gabriel	Rev. H. S. Trainor		1939	twice mthly			x	x			

[3] "We alternate, sometimes the entire Mass is recited [by the congregation] in English, and again the principal parts in Latin with the Offertory and Communion prayers in English.

CHICAGO PARISHES USING DIALOG MASS—*Continued*

Parish	Pastor	Cisca Survey 1939	Sod. Survey 1941	How long?	Sdy Chd'n	Sdy Adults	Wkly	Leader	Engl. only	Latin only	Engl.-Latin
24 St. Gall	Rev. J. D. Hishen				twice mthly				x		
25 St. George	Rev. D. A. Diederich			1920	wkly				x		
26 St. Gertrude	Msgr. J. G. Kealy			1940	occ.			x		x	
27 St. Gregory	Msgr. M. Klasen			1915	wkly	wkly		x	x		
28 St. Hedwig	Rev. F. Uzdrowski, C.R.				wkly				Polish		
29 St. Helen	Rev. P. Pyterek	x		1936	wkly			x	Polish		
30 Holy Trinity	Rev. M. G. Sesterhenn		x		wkly	wkly					x
31 St. Hyacinth	Rev. T. Kloptowski, C.R.				wkly				Polish		
32 Immac. Conc.	Rev. A. Drohan, C.P.						daily		x		
33 St. Jerome	Msgr. D. Frawley				wkly				x		
34 St. John Bosco	Rev. J. B. Sugrue		x	1937	wkly	mthly			x	x[4]	
35 St. Joseph	Rev. L. F. DeCelle		x	Nov 1940	wkly		daily conv			x	

No.	Parish	Pastor		Year							
36	St. Joseph	Rev. S. Cholewinski			wkly						
37	St. Lawrence	Rev. P. J. McGuire			wkly					x	
38	St. Ludmilla	Rev. F. Tony		1936	mthly	One Mass mthly	wkly	x			
39	St. Marg. Mary	Rev. G. T. McCarthy		1938	wkly			x	x		
40	St. Maria Incor.	Rev. J. Lazzeri, P.S.S.C.B.			wkly		daily				
41	St. Mary Magd.	Msgr. J. J. Kozlowski		1938	wkly	3 Masses	daily		Polish		
42	St. Mary, Mt. Carm.	Rev. A. Della Vecchia C.PP.S.	x		wkly						x
43	St. Michael	Rev. J. J. Saulinskas		1935	wkly		seldom			x	
44	St. Nicholas	Rev. T. Bonifas		1938		wkly			x		
45	Notre Dame	Rev. Z. Belanger, S.S.S.	x	1938	mthly	mthly		x	x		
46	O. L. Help Chr's	Msgr. R. S. Kelly	x	1936		twice mthly		x			
47	O. L. of Grace	Msgr. V. Primeau		Feb 1941	mthly					x	x

4 English form at Children's Mass, Latin at adults'.

CHICAGO PARISHES USING DIALOG MASS—Continued

Parish	Pastor	Cisca Survey 1939	Sod. Survey 1941	How long?	Sdy Chd'n	Sdy Adults	Wkly	Leader	Engl. only	Latin only	Engl.-Latin
48 O. L. of Lourdes	Rev. A. Mergl										
49 O. L. of Mercy	Msgr. W. F. Cahill	x		1920		One Mass 2mthly	two or three	x	x		
50 O. L. of Mt. Carm.	Msgr. J. A. Casey			1938	wkly				x	x[4]	
51 O. L. of Sorrows	Rev. V. Scheltinga, O.S.M.	x	x	1917	wkly	wkly	wkly	x	x		
52 St. Patrick	Rev. T. J. Hayes			1939	mthly		Lent		x	x[5]	x
53 SS. Peter & Paul	Rev. A. Terlecke			1928	occ		freq			x	
54 St. Philip Benizi	Rev. L. Giambastiani, O.S.M.				wkly						
55 St. Raphael	Rev. J. J. Schiller			1936	wkly			x	x		
56 St. Richard	Rev. F. J. Quinn	x		1932	wkly	One Mass 3 Sdys			x		

	Pastor		Date			4 days				
57 St. Rob't Bellarm	Rev. F. J. Gillespie		1931	wkly				x		
58 St. Roman	Rev. V. Belinski		1937	wkly		daily	x	Polish		
59 St. Sabina	Msgr. T. F. Egan			wkly				x		
60 St. Symphorosa	Rev. J. L. Sharp	x	1929	wkly		daily		x	x[6]	
61 St. Thomas Apos.	Msgr. T. V. Shannon	x	1937	mthly	One Mass wkly		x	x		
62 St. Thomas Aquinas	Rev. P. Long		Jan 1940		One Mass 2 mthly		x	x		
63 St. Thomas Cant.	Msgr. E. Fox			wkly			x	x		
64 St. Vitus	Rev. B. Kvitek, O.S.B.		1939		One Mass wkly	4, 5	x			x
65 (Unidentified church)			1939	twice mthly		2				x
BARRINGTON 66 St. Anne	Rev. P. J. Hayes				Lent only		x	x		

[4] English form at Children's Mass, Latin at adults'.
[5] English responses at parish Mass, Latin at school Mass.
[6] One weekday Mass with English responses, one with Latin.

Chicago Parishes Using Dialog Mass—*Continued*

Parish	Pastor	Cisca Survey 1939	Sod. Survey 1941	How long?	Sdy Chd'n	Sdy Adults	Wkly	Leader	Engl. only	Latin only	Engl.-Latin
BUFFALO GROVE 67 St. Mary	Rev. A. J. Boecker			1935			5		x		
CHICAGO HEIGHTS 68 St. Ann	Rev. C. Zeitler, O.M.C.			1940	wkly	One Mass wkly	freq		x		
69 St. Casimir	Rev. P. N. Katauskas			Mar 1941			one		x		
70 St. Paul	Rev. E. Sendek			1933			two		Slov		
71 San Rocco	Rev. P. Bonanni, O.M.C.			Oct 1940	wkly				x		
CICERO 72 O. L. of H. Mt.	Rev. A. J. Dedera		x		occ.	occ.			x[7]		
DES PLAINES 73 St. Mary	Rev. J. Linden			Dec 1940	wkly		3	x	x		
EVANSTON 74 St. Mary	Rev. F. E. Hillenbrand				wkly				x		

Parish	Pastor										
75 St. Bernardine	Rev. J. T. Wagener										
Franklin Park 76 St. Gertrude	Rev. R. E. Stoeckel		1936	wkly	One Mass mthly	daily			x		
Fremont Center 77 St. Mary	Rev. O. C. Nabholz								x		
Glen Ellyn 78 St. Petronilla	Rev. P. Engeln		1928			when poss.			x[8]		
Harvey 79 St. John Baptist	Rev. J. A. Grembowicz		1939	mthly	twice mthly		x		Polish		
Highland Park 80 Immac. Conc.	Rev. J. D. O'Neill, D.D.		1934	twice mthly	twice mthly	daily	x		x		
Homewood 81 St. Joseph	Rev. S. P. Sullivan			twice mthly						x	
Joliet 82 St. Anthony	Rev. G. A. Cloos		Apr 1941	wkly		seldom	x		x		
83 St. Joseph	Rev. J. M. Butala	x	1938	wkly					x		
84 St. Mary	Rev. A. Sinsky		1938	twice mthly		5					x

7 "The *Missa Recitata* is not practical where two languages are in use."
8 Dialog Mass on Sundays discontinued.

CHICAGO PARISHES USING DIALOG MASS—*Continued*

Parish	Pastor	Cisca Survey 1939	Sod. Survey 1941	How long?	Sdy Chd'n	Sdy Adults	Wkly	Leader	Engl. only	Latin only	Engl.-Latin
85 Sacred Heart	Rev. J. A. Keating			Feb 1941	2, 3						x
86 St. Thaddeus	Rev. J. O. Karabasz				wkly	one Mass wkly					x
LA GRANGE 87 St. Fran. Xavier	Rev. W. J. O'Brien			1938		one Mass mthly					x
LISLE 88 St. Joan of Arc	Rev. T. J. Sindelar, O.S.B.			1933	mthly		2				x
MANHATTAN 89 St. Joseph	Rev. J. I. Gallery			Apr 1940	mthly						x
MAYWOOD 90 St. Eulalia	Rev. M. E. Muzik			May 1940	mthly						x
MELROSE PARK 91 O. L. of Mt. Carm.	Rev. B. Franch, P.S.S.C.B.			1938	wkly				x		

		17	11		61	30	43	32	59	18	21
92 Sacred Heart	Rev. H. Lieblang						3				x
MOMENCE 93 St. Patrick	Rev. T. U. Demarais		x	Sept 1940	mthly		2		x		x
POSEN 94 St. Stanislaus	Rev. S. A. Rozak			Lent 1941		one Mass	Lent				
RIVER GROVE 95 St. Cyprian	Rev. G. P. Stafford			Sept 1939			2, 3	x	x		
SKOKIE 96 St. Peter	Rev. C. F. Eckert			Apr 1941			daily	x			x
TECHNY 97 St. Norbert	Rev. W. A. Binz, S.V.D.	x		1935			daily	x	x		
WAUKEGAN 98 St. Joseph	Rev. C. J. Mertens	x		1934			daily	x	x		x
99 Mother of God	Rev. M. J. Hiti			1936	wkly		2, 3				
WEST CHICAGO 100 St. Mary	Rev. F. A. McLaughlin			Sept 1940	wkly				x		
WILMETTE 101 St. Francis Xavier	Rev. M. D. McNamara			1937	twice mthly					x	
101 Churches		17	11		61	30	43	32	59	18	21

In addition to the above, the Cisca survey of 1939 listed these churches as using Dialog Mass, and there is no evidence on hand of its discontinuance:

St. Malachy, Rev. J. Brown, used on Sundays at Children's Mass;

St. Mel. Holy Ghost, Msgr. F. A. Purcell, D.D., used on Sundays at Children's Mass;

St. William, Rev. P. E. Loeffl, used on Sundays at Children's Mass.

Among the churches that reported in the official Chicago survey as about to begin the practice of the Mass in dialog one may note the following:

All Saints, Rev. G. Paskauskas: "I am most willing to introduce the Dialog Mass; please send information."

St. Barbara, Rev. S. Radniecki: "We will introduce the *Missa Recitata* in St. Barbara's Church as soon as the books come and the children are instructed. It will be on all school days and Sundays and holydays."

St. Cyril, Rev. A. Werner, O. Carm.: "Since the Carmelite Rite is somewhat different from the Roman, we are preparing a book with the prayers of our Rite in Latin and English. When that is printed we intend to use the *Missa Recitata*."

St. George, Rev. A. Madic, O.F.M.: "I would like to institute it, and will most likely do so in the near future."

Holy Rosary, Rev. U. Broccolo: "We do intend to start with the children."

St. James, Rev. E. A. Przybylski: "We are contemplating starting it next Autumn."

St. Philomena, Rev. L. H. Wand : "We are considering its use next year."

St. Martha, Morton Grove, Rev. R. H. Wilhelm : "We hope to introduce the same in the near future."

St. Joseph, Rockdale, Rev. J. Brons, O.S.B.: "Plans are already made for the introduction of Dialog Mass at the Summer School beginning June 15th. I will appreciate any guidance."

We pass at once to the data reflecting the present use of Dialog Mass in Chicagoland's educational and other institutions. These questionnaires were more completely filled in, and so the compilation affords a more accurate general picture. To begin with, one might note that, while the Sodality survey reached twenty-four out of the forty schools here reporting, it reached only eleven out of the hundred-and-one parishes now reporting the use of Dialog Mass. One might note, too, that in 37% of the institutions here reporting, the Dialog Mass is used for the religious themselves. Another angle of the survey that gives great hope for the future is the prevalence of the use of Latin, or a Latin-English combination, in Dialog Mass as now in use in Chicago's schools. The situation in the parish churches is not, in this respect, nearly so favorable, and eventual readjustment will have to be considered. For that readjustment there is this annually-increasing nucleus of the school-groups trained in the use of Latin at Dialog Mass. The tables follow:

COLLEGES, ACADEMIES, CONVENTS, INSTITUTIONS USING DIALOG MASS

Institution	1941 Sod. Survey	DM for Relig.	Mass Stud. frq.	DM Stud. frq.	How long?	Leader	Engl. only	Latin only	Engl.-Latin
1 Academy of Our Lady			15 yrly	8 or 10				x	
2 Alvernia High School	x		mthly	mthly	1930	x			x
3 Aquinas High School	x	mthly	mthly	mthly	Sept 1940	x			x
4 Bl. Agnes High School			daily	mthly	Apr 1940				x
5 De Paul University			wkly	wkly	1938			x	
6 Holy Family Academy	x	mthly	mthly	mthly	Oct 1940				x
7 Holy Trinity High School			3, 4 yrly	once		x		x	
8 Immaculata High	x		9 yrly	9 yrly	1936	x			x
9 Institute of B. V. Mary		daily	mthly	retr mthly		x			x
10 Josephinum High School	x	Sdys feasts	retr mthly	mthly	1937	x		x	

#	School	Col 1	Col 2	Col 3	Col 4	Col 5	Col 6	Col 7	Col 8
12	Lourdes High School	x	mthly	retr mthly					x
13	Loyola Academy		daily	retr daily	1937	x			x
14	Loyola University	x	wkly	wkly	Sept 1940	x			x
15	Mercy High School	x	mthly	mthly	Oct 1940			x	
16	Notre Dame High School	x	7 yrly	7 yrly	1939	x			x
17	Providence High School	x	7 yrly	6 yrly	1931	x			x
18	Resurrection High School	x	mthly	mthly	Dec 1940			x	
19	Sacred Heart Convent	x	wkly	wkly	1931			x	
20	St. Casimer Academy	x	mthly	mthly	1938				x
21	St. Ignatius High School		daily	twice wkly			x⁹		
22	St. Mary High School	x	4 wkly	7 yrly	1937	x		x	
23	St. Patrick's Girls High School		mthly	mthly	1938	x			x
24	St. Philip High School	x	wkly	wkly	1937	x			x

9 "Prayers in the spirit of the Mass are recited."

COLLEGES, ACADEMIES, CONVENTS, INSTITUTIONS USING DIALOG MASS—*Continued*

Institution	1941 Sod. Survey	DM for Relig.	Mass Stud. frq.	DM Stud. frq.	How long?	Leader	Engl. only	Latin only	Engl.-Latin
25 St. Scholastica	x	daily	2 mthly	2 mthly	1930	x		x	x[10]
26 St. Sebastian Commercial High School			wkly	wkly	1925		x		
27 Siena High School		daily	mthly	mthly	1939			x	
28 Trinity High School	x		wkly	wkly				x	
DES PLAINES 29 St. Patrick's Academy	x		mthly	mthly	1937			x	
EVANSTON 30 Marywood School		daily	3 wkly	3 wkly	1937			x	
JOLIET 31 Catholic High School			wkly	mthly	1939	x			x
32 College of St. Francis & Academy	x		daily	occ.		x			x
LA GRANGE 33 Nazareth Academy		daily	2 wkly	2 wkly	1938				x
LAKE FOREST 34 Barat College of S. Heart	x	wkly	daily	wkly	1938				x

36 St. Procopius College & Academy	x		daily	2 wkly	1925	x			x
MOMENCE 37 St. Patrick's Academy	x	2 wkly	daily	2 wkly	1936				x
RIVER FOREST 38 Trinity High School			mthly	mthly	1938		x		
WAUKEGAN 39 Holy Child High School			9 yrly	9 yrly	1937				x
WILMETTE 40 Mallinckrodt High School	x		2 mthly	2 mthly	1931	x	x		x
CHICAGO 41 St. Thomas Apostle Convent		wkly	wkly	mthly	Dec 1940		x		
42 Lewis Memorial Maternity Hospital		daily			1938				x
43 Angel Guardian Orphanage					1936			x	
44 Cenacle Convent		wkly					x	x	
45 Guardian Angel Home				5 wkly[11]			x		

[10] Latin only for the religious, English-Latin for students: Leader used at students' Mass only.
[11] "Starting in September."

166 THE DIALOG MASS

COLLEGES, ACADEMIES, CONVENTS, INSTITUTIONS USING DIALOG MASS—*Continued*

Institution	1941 Sod. Survey	DM for Relig.	Mass Stud. frq.	DM Stud. frq.	How long?	Leader	Engl. only	Latin only	Engl.-Latin
46 St. Mary of Providence Institute		daily	daily	daily	1926		x		
JOLIET 47 St. Joseph Hospital		daily	wkly	wkly	1936			x	
LEMONT 48 Mt. Assisi Convent		daily			1938	x			
LISLE 49 St. Joseph Orphanage				wkly	May 1940		x		
MUNDELEIN 50 Our Lady of Lake Seminary			daily	daily	1938			x	
TECHNY 51 Holy Ghost Convent & Academy	x			wkly	1938			x	
WARRENVILLE 52 Cenacle Convent		daily	during retreat	during retreat	Sept 1940			x	
53 St. Mary (?) Unidentified Institution			wkly	wkly	1939				
54 St. Mary (?) Unidentified Institution		mthly			1936			x	
Total: 54 Institutions (40 colleges, high schools)	24	20				20	5	22	25

It had been hoped to get an accurate record of when Dialog Mass was begun in each parish and institution, but that question went unanswered in most cases. Still the data supplied enable one to point out the parallelism of the graphs below. It is a neat instance, we believe, of one and the same spirit (and Spirit) working itself out in differing spheres of influence.

Non-parochial Academies, Institutions, etc.		Parish Churches	
Up to 1930 inc.	6	Up to 1930 inc.	7
1931–1935	4	1931–1935	11
1936	5	1936	6
1937	7	1937	5
1938	9	1938	11
1939	4	1939	8
1940	9	1940	14
		1941 (to May)	7

The upswing for 1940 is due both to the new Ordinary's direct interest and the manifold discussion of Dialog Mass at the First National Liturgical Week, held in Chicago, October 1940. This "decade of progress" indicates a natural curve, always true of the workings of that Spirit which reaches from end to end mightily and accomplishes things *sweetly*.

One hundred and one Chicago churches now report the use of Dialog Mass. The sodalists' survey tabulated only eleven of these; just as in the Diocese of La Crosse it reached only twelve out of true total of eighty-six. These facts indicate that the true incidence of Dialog Mass the country over is vastly greater than indicated in the Sodality survey. The Chicago total is roughly one-fourth (23.49%) of the total number of churches in the Archdiocese. Thus, in a decade, with episcopal initiative only during the last year and a half, Dialog Mass won entry into one out of every four churches in the nation's most populous diocese.

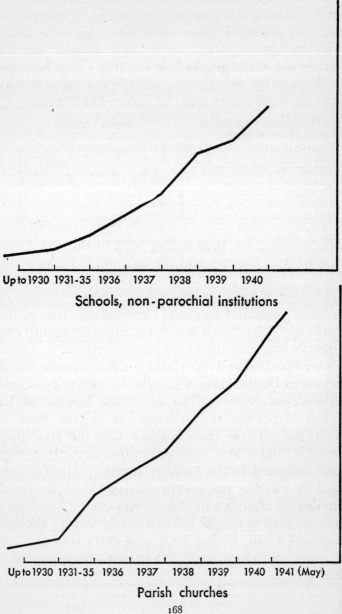

Schools, non-parochial institutions

Parish churches

The Cisca survey of 1939 had twenty-eight churches where Dialog Mass was held for the children, only four where it was also for adults: this is in the ratio of *seven to one*. Dialog Mass in the parish churches is still predominantly for the children. In the present official survey forty-one churches list it for children, Sundays only, and thirteen others as for children on weekdays only. Some churches do not indicate the composition of the congregation at Dialog Mass, but no less than twenty-nine churches list it on Sundays for adult congregations: this is a little short of the ratio of *three to one*. This spells progress far more rapid than might have been thought possible. In Chicago, and La Crosse, and elsewhere, Dialog Mass will soon cease to connote a youth exercise.

With the passing of what we might call the 'youth phase' of Dialog Mass, the question of the language used will demand reexamination. In Chicagoland at present our incomplete returns break down as follows:

Latin only .... 18 churches
English-Latin .... 21 churches
Vernacular only .... 59 churches

Answers made to the celebrant are intended to be in Latin: "Besides joining the server in the Latin responses," is the phrase of the pertinent part of Archbishop Stritch's regulation of June 1940. That important document is cited elsewhere in this volume, but for completeness' sake it is herewith repeated:

THE *MISSA RECITATA*

"This *Missa Recitata,* concerning which the S. C. R., explicitly legislated, and as it is universally celebrated, consists in its minimum form, in the congregation joining the server in his responses; in its more expanded form, also explicitly approved, the congregation, besides joining the server in the Latin responses, also recites with the celebrant the Ordinary parts of the Mass which in a *Missa Cantata* are intended to be sung by the congregation: i.e., the *Gloria, Credo, Sanctus* (and *Benedictus*), and *Agnus Dei*. Frequently added are the *Confiteor* and triple *Domine non sum dignus* immediately before the people's Communion.

"This is the method approved according to the mind of the Most Reverend Samuel A. Stritch, Archbishop of Chicago."

By the English-Latin form mentioned in the above tabulation is meant the limiting of English to such parts as are not recited *aloud* by the priest, such as Offertory prayers and prayers before Communion. One may remit further consideration of this thorny problem of language to the next chapter, with a reference to the form there given and used in the Cathedral of Peoria.

This Chancery survey also serves to illustrate the greater 'traditionalism' of the religious orders in two respects. First, Dialog Mass is listed as a part of the daily life of seminarians at the great diocesan St. Mary of the Lake Seminary at Mundelein, but is not reported for any of the twelve seminaries for religious in the Archdiocese. Again, in the matter of parish churches administered by the religious clergy we find this engaging cross-cut statistic:

A. Religious priests using Dialog Mass in parish churches
.... Blessed Sacrament Fathers, Passionists, Precious Blood, Society of Divine Word;

B. Religious priests not using
   Dialog Mass in parish
   churches ....Augustinians, Dominicans,
                           Holy Cross, Jesuits, Paulists,
                           Viatorians ;
C. Religious priests using Dialog Mass in some churches,
   not in others ....Benedictines, Carmelites, Fran-
                           ciscans, Missionaries of St.
                           Charles, Redemptorists, Resur-
                           rectionists and Servites.

At the conclusion of the survey the mind recalls with gratitude words addressed by Archbishop Stritch to the participants in Liturgical Week, and finds them applicable also to the present work accomplished under His Excellency's own directions: "We are proud and glad that this Archdiocese . . . has contributed notably to the furtherance of that noble work of the liturgical revival. . . For is it not tremendously inspiriting, in these sad and tragic days, to behold with our bodily eyes, as well as with the eyes of faith, the glorious spectacle of the Church at prayer, and to join with her in psalms and hymns and canticles as she offers a fitting worship, a 'clean oblation' to the eternal Father of us all? . . . The Catholic body of this Archdiocese has received a new impetus to know and live with Christ in His Church, and to translate that knowledge into action truly Christlike and Catholic."

Such becomes the citizens of that no mean city, the heart of Mid-America.

CHAPTER IX

CHILDREN'S DIALOG MASS: SIX METHODS

Dialog Mass has come as a boundless comfort for all concerned in a great many churches long familiar with this situation described by a recent correspondent in *America*: "At the children's Masses all we can see is one Sister in each section spending most of the precious time during Mass hauling Jack out of the seat next to Fred and forcing him to sit next to Bill."[1]   In fact, in the United States, up to now, Dialog Mass is thought of as predominantly a practice for the young. Dialog Mass in itself is something principally for the adult, and when handed down to the young, it must, like everything else for children, be accommodated to ages and capacities.

Children are different (profound observation!) from adults, not only in their capacities, but in their reactions and motivations: how many children, for instance, eat their spinach with an eye on the dessert, for 'mixed' motives?   Children are naturally restless, incapable of sustained endeavor.   Again, children, as they grow, feel themselves progressively different from other children, and while they do not mind being treated like those a little older than themselves, they most bitterly resent being treated like those younger. Where children ranging all the way from seven to thirteen, roughly from the third to the eighth grades, all attend one and the same Mass in a body, this vast

[1] *America*, LXIV, 22 (March 8, 1941), 605.

difference imposes on those charged with their religious formation a problem almost as complex as it is important. The method, or methods, adopted must be sufficiently easy so that those at the lowest end of the scale can be interested and engaged, and sufficiently mature so that those at the upper end can find therein the basis for life-long habits. And since the external activity, by which participants may join with the priest in the Sacrifice, is so narrowly circumscribed, every possible avenue that is open, or 'openable,' to interest, to understanding, to cooperation, must be utilized to the full. Rev. J. T. McMahon, of South Perth, Australia, said in this connection some time ago: "In recent years much attention is given in liturgical publications to the Dialog Mass. The principle of the Dialog Mass is that children and people learn by doing. . . . We must look on it [the Mass] as an Action in which we, and the children we teach, are to participate. The liturgy teaches through experience, through cooperation, through action. . . . We are called upon to do something, and the doing inspires thought. We act to think, we act to learn, we act to live the Mass." [2] The Dialog Mass for children, then, must be a combination of silent prayer, of recited prayer, of reading and of song, and the whole calculated to enable all participants, from seven to thirteen or older, to join with the priest in giving, or offering Sacrifice, and join with the priest in getting, or in completing the Sacrifice by "eating of the Sacrifice," (I Cor. x, 18), sacramentally or spiritually.

However arranged, Dialog Mass would be disastrous if it allowed no time for silent, individual prayer.

[2] J. T. McMahon, "Teaching the Mass to Children," *American Ecclesiastical Review*, XCVII, 5 (Nov. 1937), 427-34.

Even young children must be taught to pray in un-studied directness and simplicity — and privacy. The fact that children find praying hard must not lead us to deprive them of these intervals, however short, for personal converse with our common Father in Heaven. Instruction classes should teach the children how to use these intervals, with or without a fixed text, and the Mass, we repeat, must provide such silent-periods. The Canon of the Mass, it might be noted, may not be prayed aloud in any language, by any age-group, old or young : this is a papal prohibition. Since the prayers recited by priest and server at the foot of the altar are the very hardest in the entire Mass to pray collectively, the Dialog Mass for children very often begins communal prayer at the *Kyrie*.

The mention of communal prayer and the *Kyrie* brings us face to face with one of the biggest factors of the whole problem, that of language, used here in the sense of a tongue. The Roman Mass, as we have it, is a mixture of languages, inasmuch as the text, for the most part Latin, admits some Greek (*Kyrie eleison, Christe eleison*) and a few Hebrew words such as *Amen, Alleluia, Sabbaoth, Hosanna.* Now, such very short responses as *Amen* (Hebrew), *Deo gratias, Et cum spiritu tuo, Laus tibi Christe* (Latin) and *Kyrie eleison, Christe eleison* (Greek) can be learned in meaning and expression about as quickly in the original as in a translation. The framework of communal participation of children with the Action of the priest lies in this very series of short responses said in unison with the server. Apart from the prayers at the foot of the altar, *Et cum spiritu tuo* occurs eight times in the course of the Mass, at the introduction to nearly each important episode, Collect (s) , Gospel, Offertory, Pref-

ace-Canon, *Pax,* Post-Communion, Blessing, Last
Gospel. Saying it gives all, the youngest included,
eight chances to voice participation with priest and all
other worshipers. Then there is *Amen,* which, as a
response, occurs at the end of the Collect(s), Secret(s),
Canon, Breaking of Host, at the absolution-forms after
the *Confiteor,* after the Post-Communion(s) and the
Blessing: thus it provides eight more easy links with
the altar and the group. *Deo gratias* occurs at the end
of the Epistle and Last Gospel, and before the Blessing. If to the foregoing are added the few short items
*Gloria tibi Domine, Laus tibi Christe, Habemus ad
Dominum* and *Dignum et iustum est,* it will be found
that, barring the *Iudica* and *Suscipiat,* all the servers'
responses can easily be placed into the mouths of the
entire group of worshipers. This gives, then, as an
elementary scheme:

Et cum spiritu tuo ....eight responses
Amen ....eight responses
Kyrie eleison, Christe eleison ....four responses
Deo gratias ....three responses
Gloria tibi Domine, Laus tibi Christe ....two responses
Dignum et iustum est ....one response
Habemus ad Dominum ....one response

twenty-seven responses

These last two, of course, are taken into the scheme to
enable the group to go through the entire dialog before the Preface-Canon.

In proportion as younger children, of the ages of
seven to nine, may regularly predominate in the grouping at the Children's Mass, not much more responding,
and little communal recitation can be thought of. If
children of ten to thirteen make up the majority of

the worshipers, the joint-recitation characteristic of the adults' Dialog Mass can be developed a little at a time, and used as circumstances dictate. The shorter elements, such as the *Agnus Dei,* the *Sanctus-Benedictus* and *Domine non sum dignus,* are the easier and can be managed with no great effort. To achieve the smooth, rhythmic, and not-too-slow recitation of the *Gloria* and *Credo* might seem in theory to be very difficult; but those are the years when children's memories are like wax, and their gift of imitative expression at its zenith. The wise director will be careful, however, not to allow the needs of the younger children to be drowned in these deeper waters of Latin-language praying of their older associates. "Formerly in English, now in Latin," was a notation that occurred several times on the returns of the sodalists' Dialog Mass survey. "In English at present, later, we hope, in Latin," is an echo of the foregoing with only a change of tense. "The Latin form on Tuesday and Saturday, the English form on Wednesday and Thursday," was the jotting on another letter. Of course the answers made to the priest must be made in Latin, but that taken care of, a good many churches now have some of the other parts, such as the *Gloria* and *Credo,* recited at first in English, by the entire group as a unit, or split into two choirs each answering the other.

Besides the question of the Latin or the vernacular, there is for younger children the problem of *vocabulary.* The wording of the missal prayers is too long and too difficult for the younger tots. Prayers must be given in words and word-groups that carry a correct and direct message to their opening minds. A missal prepared for adults or adolescents is by that very fact obviously unsuited to young children.

To be added, then, with older children, as circumstances allow:

Agnus Dei (entire or just *miserere nobis, dona nobis pacem*)
Domine non sum dignus (entire) before the people's Communion
Sanctus-Benedictus
Credo
Confiteor
Suscipiat
Introibo-Iudica

There remains the question of the use of a 'leader' whose part it is to start the prayers, to read in the vernacular some of the Ordinary of the day. The ideal leader is a priest, and where the number of the clergy so permits, one often finds a priest acting in this capacity. The vernacular rendering of Collect, Epistle, Gospel and Post-Communion may be thus added to the scope of the Dialog Mass features. Later, the choral elements, Introit, Gradual, Offertory Verse and Communion Verse may round out the leader's assignments.

To the foregoing one must add the very widespread usage of having the entire congregation recite in unison some of the Offertory prayers, as well as prayers before and after Communion. In the sodalists' survey it was disclosed that this feature is universally popular in every corner of the country.

The Reverend George Zimpfer, of Williamsville (Diocese of Buffalo), attributes success in introducing the Dialog Mass to the patience that is satisfied at first with a small and humble beginning.[3] His plan starts by having the *altar-boys,* not two or four, but twenty

[3] G. Zimpfer, "Presenting the 'Dialog Mass,'" *Homiletic and Pastoral Review*, XLI, 9 (June, 1941), 898-903: quoted above with permission.

or thirty, recite together. "This practice," he says, "is not only edifying to the people, but it effectively checks the slovenly recitation which is so common. The rhythm of the Latin becomes apparent to the group, the pauses are more carefully observed, and if one here and there is tempted to speed, he is noticed at once—and corrected." Let Father Zimpfer outline the succeeding steps of his procedure:

"Now that a nucleus has been formed, the next step is to go into the classrooms (not at a general assembly), and explain in simple terms that the priest wants the help of many for a project very dear to him. He wants boys and girls who will pray the Mass *with him* at least once a week. If any tyke rises and asks how this may be done, the priest calms his or her fears by saying that he himself will do all the teaching, very gradually, *in church each morning before Mass.* There won't be any extra studying! This is going to be learning to pray the Mass with the priest because that is the best way to love and understand the Mass. The priest may explain, too, that he feels it isn't right that he should be, as it were, separated from his people when he is offering Mass, that the early Christians always prayed with their priests at Mass, and were attentive because they understood what was going on. They didn't just watch—and dream. . .

"The experiment begins the next morning. The sacristy bell rings promptly and you approach the altar with your full escort of altar-boys. You arrange the chalice and Missal, descend—and go to the Communion-rail for your first liturgical talk to your new society which is assembled in the front pews of the middle aisle. The talk should not last more than five minutes. As a preliminary you open the box of

*Community Mass** booklets which you have previously placed at the rail, and each member, altar-boys included, receives one. You explain that you are not going to ask the members to learn any Latin prayers, for that service is reserved to the altar-boys, but that each week you will ask them to recite one or two prayers in common. The selection of these prayers from the Ordinary of the Mass may be left, of course, to the discretion of the Moderator, but it is advisable to begin with the *Gloria* and the *Credo*. Each morning, to each successive group, the priest gives the same basic instruction as to the manner of this praying-in-common. . .

"With the Monday of each week comes a new venture, a new lesson, and this includes of course what has already been learned. The second week may be devoted to the first two prayers of the Offertory; the week following to the Offering of the Chalice and the prayer, 'Accept, O Holy Trinity' (omitting the *Lavabo*). Excluding the Canon, as liturgical regulations demand, the next week's talks could explain the proper recital of the 'Our Father.' Then could come the three prayers before Communion, which easily surpass anything the ordinary prayerbook can supply as adequate preparation for the reception of the Sacrament. These prayers of the Ordinary are *introduced* during the Mass by an appointed 'leader,' boy or girl, after which introduction the group prays in unison.

"As soon as the 'technique' of the Ordinary has been grasped, the Moderator selects alert and interested girls and boys who may each day assume the duty of 'reader' of the Proper. Each morning these two

* Excellent and practical copies are supplied by *The Queen's Work*, 3742 West Pine Boulevard, St. Louis.

appointments are made, that of the 'leader' of the Ordinary and that of the 'reader' of the Proper. As the weeks pass, one after another of the Proper parts is explained to the group in general and to the reader in particular. Moderators will wisely choose the Gospel to be first read, since it is the best-known. The Epistle and Preface may follow, and towards the end the more difficult Collects, Secrets and Post-Communions may be included. . .

"Now what is the effect of all this upon the adults? The answer is that they are delighted and impressed. If they are encouraged to take their places directly behind the children and to use the booklets, they soon become enthusiastic and regular participants of the 'Dialogue Mass.' The writer conducts his 'Dialogue Mass' at 7 a.m. daily except Saturdays. The average weekly attendance is about 80, but has risen as high as 105, not including the adults. But the adults attend this Mass in far greater numbers than before, and they almost invariably receive Communion with the children. Another important point to be noted is that both adults and children gradually become interested in the *Daily* Missal and desire to possess one. They feel they have graduated from the Sunday Missal! Left to themselves, children use the Missal only in a haphazard and irregular manner. Using it with a group makes the reading intelligible and interesting. . . .

"The task, instead of being difficult, will soon 'sell itself' to any priest who gives it a fair trial."

The special interest of this quotation obviates the need of excuse for the length of the citations.

Lastly, there is the all-important factor of song, and its proper place in the Dialog Mass. The Holy See

BISHOP SCHULTE CELEBRATING DIALOG MASS

"We Welcome Dialog Mass to the Diocese of Leavenworth"

has for Rome regulated and enumerated the time-periods when singing may be used at high Mass and at low Mass. Dialog Mass, I take it, is a low Mass, and as such falls within the restrictions thus phrased by the Cardinal-Vicar *for Rome* under Pope Pius X: "During low Masses motets may be sung, and the organ be played, as the rite permits. It is, however, important to observe the rule that voices and organ shall only be heard during those times when the priest is not reciting aloud, viz., besides the time of Preparation and Thanksgiving, from the *Offertory* to the *Preface,* from the *Sanctus* to the *Pater* and from the *Agnus* to the *Post-Communion,* the singing being suspended if Holy Communion be given for the recital of the *Confiteor* and the *Ecce Agnus Dei*." [4]

The Church recommends a hymn right before Mass (priest's preparation). No better psychological 'tuning in' process is to be found than a brisk, short song. It can be chosen as an overture, so to speak, to throw into relief the dominant sentiment of the season, Advent, Christmastide, Lent, Paschaltide, time after Pentecost, or to characterize the Saint of the day, a martyr, a confessor, a virgin, a widow, and so forth.

Again there is a short space available for song between the Offertory versicle and the beginning of the Preface. As this is, in sacrificial worship, the inauguration of one of the principal phases of the entire rite, it is eminently fitting that prayer at this high point be sung to God. By the same token it is demanded that *what is sung* be an idea belonging to the Mass, and even to this very part of the Mass, which is that of giving, offering, giving of self under tokens of bread

[4] Letter of Cardinal Vicar, Feb. 2, 1912: English version in *Catholic Church Music* (London: Burns, Oates & Washbourne, 1933), 31.

and wine in union with Christ's great Gift to be.   An
unrelated hymn, however pious in itself, is merely an
officially imposed distraction just at the moment when
one is most in need of fullest attention.   "Sing the
Mass, don't just sing during Mass," the famous dictum
of Pope Pius X, was pronounced with a restoration of
congregationally-sung high Mass in view, but it has
its own logical application to the Dialog Mass as well.
The ideal and inexhaustible theme of Offertory hymns
is embedded in that Offertory prayer first prayed under
such dramatic circumstances by the direct inspiration
of the Holy Spirit : "In a humble spirit and a contrite
heart may we be received by Thee, O Lord, and may
our Sacrifice so be offered in Thy sight this day, that
it may be pleasing to Thee, O Lord God" (cf. Daniel
iii, 39, 40) .

Again, if song is used between the Consecration and
the *Pater noster,* as is permitted, it is equally imper-
ative that the theme of the song be one that will make
it easier, not harder, to keep one's mind on the Sacrifice in progress on the altar.   In this connection let us
recall that direct adoration of Christ's presence on the
altar, (except in the moment of the Elevation), is not
what the Church dwells on in the prayers after the
Consecration : she is still concerned with giving a now
All-Perfect Gift.   Who will turn the *Per ipsum* and
its inexhaustible connotations into a moving Mass-
hymn that millions of Catholics might sing at this
climax of the Mass rite?

Century after century Christians came to Communion singing, and receded from the Table of the
Lord singing their love of God in Christ Jesus our
Lord.   The Church still suggests the time of the distribution of Communion for song.   Lastly, she sug-

gests a song at the very end, during the fleeting moment of thanksgiving: song, feels our holy Mother,
the hierarchical Church, is the very best way to close
that communal worship Action that is the Mass.

It will not be out of place to repeat once more that
children will like Dialog Mass for what may seem to
adults the 'wrong' reasons. Let us rather say *children's reasons,* which are not at all the ultimate ones
the Church has in mind in urging Dialog Mass on
adult congregations. The Dialog Mass appeals to
children because it engages them, gives them a part,
answers their basic need to be doing something.
"Years ago, when I was a boy," I recall a man telling
me, in a country where the liturgical movement is
much older than amongst us, "I liked the Dialog Mass
because it made the Mass go faster: then, little by
little, I learned I was having a part in the Church's
worldwide, Heaven-wide worship, and now I want to
have my part in that chorus before God." Children's
Mass-worship, adults may fretfully feel, is so deficient:
we try so hard to teach them, and they learn so little
and so slowly. Rather let us say their Mass-worship
is child-like, after the manner of a child. "When I
was a child," it is the great St. Paul speaking, "I spoke
as a child, I felt as a child, I thought as a child; now
that I am become a man, I have made an end of child-
ish ways" (I Cor. xiii, 11). If the worship-habits we
give the children are correct, however much after the
manner of a child, we can leave the adjustments of the
future to the developing man or woman in the child.

"To succeed requires a lot of patience," writes a
South Dakota pastor of the Dialog Mass. "I know of
parishes and parish high schools that have given up
the Dialog Mass because 'it wasn't a success'—after

two or three weeks ! From the very beginning of introducing Dialog Mass into my church three years ago,
the results were gratifying. The second year was better than the first ; naturally. This year, our third, the
results are not very satisfactory from a critical listener's
position, chiefly because we have grown to expect expert mature perfection. But because an adult listener
finds the 'leading' [of the student reader] faulty is no
proof that the pupils and adults are not profiting from
this method of following the Mass. My men tell me
they are getting more out of the Mass than they ever
thought was possible. If ever a game was worth the
candle, this one is !" he ends with conviction.

The role naturally falling to the sodality or other
organized youth group in inducting the parish into the
use of the Dialog Mass, so to speak, is here uncon-
sciously expressed in a letter from a pastor's secretary :

"The Dialog Mass is used in our church on Sundays
at the children's Mass only. In unison with the altar
boys, the children say the complete Mass responses in
Latin, using a *Sunday Missal*.

"It is the desire of our pastor, the Rt. Rev. Monsignor ———, to have the entire congregation, in due
time, say the responses, at all low Masses. Monsignor
expressed the opinion that perhaps the Blessed Virgin
Mary Sodality would act as a nucleus in carrying this
plan through."

This would be a natural place to examine the reasons now preventing many spiritual directors from having the Dialog Mass. There is, first, the fear that this
Mass cannot be made to go well without frequent occurrence and much practice. "Circumstances make it
impossible for us to have Mass [for the students] more

than once a month, and we do not use the Dialog Mass because it would necessitate practice and time [for preparation]," is the way this objection was phrased by one correspondent. Of course, the sudden introduction of Dialog Mass in its fullest form would require some careful behind-the-scenes preparation; but its inauguration in the simplest form takes little more than an announcement. Once begun, its subsequent development is so spontaneous and natural that the little extra time involved will not likely be a hindrance. Perhaps the majority of day-schools in the larger cities have student Masses only once a month, as on the First Fridays: scores and scores of them have Dialog Masses under those conditions.

"Our church so far has all high Masses, and therefore we have not made any attempt at the Dialog Mass," the words come from a large Midwestern city, the sentiment is found on all sides. The relation of Dialog Mass to high Mass is very important, and in theory is to be judged by that dictum of Pope Pius XI: "The faithful come to church in order to derive piety from its chief source, by taking an active part in the venerated Mysteries, and the public, solemn prayers of the Church." [5] Therefore, in theory, the choice between high Mass and Dialog Mass cannot overlook the factor of maximum lay participation. Pius XI himself applied the principle in the same document to the Church's ideal, the high Mass congregationally sung: "In order that the faithful may more actively participate in divine worship, let them be made once more to sing the Gregorian chant, as far as it belongs to them to take part in it. It is most important that

5 Pius XI, *On Divine Worship* (Dec. 28, 1928): *Catholic Church Music* (London: Burns Oates & Washbourne, 1933), 37.

when the faithful assist at the sacred ceremonies, or when pious sodalities take part with the clergy in a procession, they should not be merely detached and silent spectators, but, filled with a deep sense of the beauty of the liturgy, they should sing alternately with the clergy and choir, as it is prescribed." [6] I do not think there is any doubt as to how the Supreme Pontiff would apply the principle of maximum active lay participation as between a weekday high Mass sung by only one (or a few), and at which five hundred children assist as "detached and silent spectators," and a Dialog Mass in which those five hundred voices *socia exsultatione concelebrant*. So, the explanation, "We do not have Dialog Mass because the children assist at high Mass every day," is the most desirable one if the children sing; not desirable, on the score of active lay participation, if their assistance is that of passive spectators.

The fear, lastly, that Dialog Mass will lead to abuses, and in some unforeseen way get out of hand, is felt often enough to warrant one's saying a word about it. The objection is more often urged against Dialog Mass for the adult congregation, but we advert to it here once and for all. In the last few years I have read literally hundreds of accounts of Dialog Mass as it is being practiced in this country. *The almost total absence of exaggerations in this novel method of Mass-worship is a tribute to the vigilance of bishops and pastors, and to the sound, trust-worthy instinct of the Catholic laity.* The Holy See has characterized the loud recitation of the Canon as an abuse : One diocese excepted, where this has now been corrected, I re-

6 Pius XI, *On Divine Worship* (Dec. 28, 1928): *Catholic Church Music* (London: Burns Oates & Washbourne, 1933), 43.

member only one instance where this was being done (*Missa complicata,* it was designated by my correspondent). Abuse is a very negligible danger. Some mistakes are humanly unavoidable : is there any priest who never makes a slip at Mass? I recall the words of a woman whose parish had gradually mastered the Dialog Mass at all low Masses : "Yes, but there were days when we could not have been proud of our performance before visitors from other parishes. The boys [leaders] made mistakes, we made mistakes, it wouldn't have been very surprising if even the priest had said the wrong prayer !"

We append to this chapter an outline of six variations of Dialog Mass. They seek to provide for feasts and occasions of differing degrees of solemnity in the matter of vocal participation in low Mass, and are calculated to lead naturally to the congregational singing at high Mass.

FIRST METHOD	SECOND METHOD
Appropriate for "purple" or "black" Masses, penance days:	Appropriate for feasts of the simple rite :
RECITATION :	RECITATION :
Kyrie eleison, Christe eleison	All in First Method, plus :
Et cum spiritu tuo	*Suscipiat Dominus*
Deo gratias	*Agnus Dei* (either entire, or
Levate	*miserere nobis, dona nobis*
Habemus ad Dominum	*pacem*)
Dignum et iustum est	

READING, English, in unison:
At Offertory:
Accept (*Suscipe*)
We offer unto Thee (*Offerimus*)
Before Communion:
O Lord, . . . Who didst say

After Communion:

May Thy Body (*Corpus tuum*)
SINGING, none

READING, English, in unison:
At Offertory:
Accept (*Suscipe*)

Before Communion:
O Lord, . . . who didst say
O Lord, . . . Son of living God
After Communion:
Into a pure heart (*Quod ore*)
May Thy Body (*Corpus tuum*)
SINGING
Hymn before Mass: of day, of season, of Saint.
Hymn, of self-offering at Offertory, after the Accept (*Suscipe*)

THIRD METHOD

Appropriate for feasts of the semidouble rite:
RECITATION:
All in Second Method, plus:
Gloria
Sanctus-Benedictus
Confiteor at Communion
READING:
All in Second Method, plus:
By Leader:
Collect, Epistle, Gospel, Post-Communion

FOURTH METHOD

Appropriate for feasts of the double rite:
RECITATION:
All in Third Method, plus:
Iudica, Introibo
Credo (if occurring)

READING:
All in Third Method, plus:
By Leader:
Introit, Gradual, Offertory Verse, Communion Verse

SINGING:
> Hymn before Mass, as in Second Method
> Hymn at Offertory, as in Second Method, after the Accept (*Suscipe*)
> Hymn during distribution of Communion

SINGING:
> Hymn before Mass, as in Second Method
> Hymn at Offertory, as in Second Method, after the Accept (*Suscipe*)
> Hymn during distribution of Communion
> Hymn during the Thanksgiving

FIFTH METHOD

Appropriate for feasts of greater double rite, or such occasions at First Fridays:

RECITATION:
> All as in Fourth Method, except *Sanctus* and *Agnus Dei*; plus, at Offertory:
> O God, Who (*Deus qui*)
> We offer unto Thee (*Offerimus*)
> In a humble spirit (*In spiritu*)

READING:
> All as in Fourth Method

SINGING:
> Chanting, *Sanctus-Benedictus, Agnus Dei, after* the priest recites them
> Hymn, during Thanksgiving

SIXTH METHOD

Appropriate for feasts of doubles of the second class:

RECITATION:
> All as in Fifth Method

READING:
> All as in Fifth Method, except Offertory prayers, and prayers before Communion

SINGING:
> Chanting, Offertory Verse, *Sanctus-Benedictus, Agnus Dei,* Communion Verse, *after* the priest recites them
> Hymn, during Thanksgiving

CHAPTER X

THE ADULT CONGREGATION: PRACTICAL SUGGESTIONS

The "trend toward Dialog Mass increases in the Catholic Church. . . [It] has already taken firm hold in Belgium, France, and the American Midwest," stated an article on the subject in the February 17, 1941, issue of *Newsweek* magazine. Prescinding from the statement about mid-America for the moment, it is clear that the appearance of such an article in that setting gives clear evidence of a stirring of increased interest in Dialog Mass in the magazine's place of origin. Other indications converge to that conclusion. A clerical correspondent in New York wrote me under date of February 24 of this year: "On Saturday I heard a very interesting lecture by Father Damasus Winzen, O.S.B., before the Association of Catholic Classical Teachers in this city. . . He gave a splendid explanation of the Dialog Mass. The interest therein is very rapidly growing in this city." Again, Emanuel A. Romero in the course of an article on "The Liturgy and the Negro Catholic," in the February issue of *Interracial Review,* passes from the discussion of theory to that of local New York practice in this fashion:

"The *Missa Recitata* (Dialog or Community Mass), in which the congregation joins in saying the prayers during the Mass, is being introduced more and more frequently throughout the country. The modern

promotion of the Dialog Mass dates back as far as
1909. . . It became known as 'the people's Mass,'
and 'the Mass with the layman's voice.' It received
its greatest impetus during the pontificate of Pius XI.
. . . It received a very great impetus at the National
Liturgical Congress held in Chicago in October, 1940.
Since Archbishop Spellman was invested with the See
of New York a noticeable increase in its use is observed. Instruction in this mode of assisting at Mass
is answering many of the longings of those who want
to know and understand more about the Catholic religion than they now do. The Catholic Laymen's
Union of New York sponsors a bi-monthly Interracial
Mass at Old St. Peter's Church in Barclay Street.
Those who have attended the Mass and joined in the
Missa Recitata have a better appreciation of the beauty
of the Mass and its place in the Liturgy of the
Church." [1]

It is a neat coincidence that the letter from which
excerpts are now offered was written in the same city
during that same week:

"It interested me to read [in the French edition of
Father Stedman's Missal] about *'la Messe dialoguée.'*
Did I ever tell you about the Mass at which I assisted
on Sunday, July 16, 1939, in the church on Mont-St.-
Michel, that unique isle off the coast of France? So
many of my richest spiritual experiences are associated
with France! I think that Mass was the holiest of my
life.

"It was *'une Messe dialoguée.'* A priest, quietly
walking up and down the center aisle, read aloud, in a
low voice, in French, in union with the priest offering
the Mass upon the altar. The congregation read from

1 *Interracial Review*, XIV, 2 (February, 1941), 26.

missals, found in the pews, and recited the responses aloud. Both priests distributed Holy Communion *at the Communion,* and it seemed as if everyone in the church approached the altar. The Mass was not interrupted for any announcements. . . ."

A further extract from this letter will be given farther on in this chapter.

When the president of a parish Catholic Action Club in a large Massachusetts city saw an item about Dialog Mass in a New York newspaper, he promptly wrote as follows:

"Dear Father: A Mass in dialog, as outlined in a news item in the New York *Herald Tribune* is of interest to me.

"This active participation and oral recitation of parts of the Mass by participants is something that warrants our attention, if we are to continue a strong and mutual interest in our faith.

"I would like to have as complete as possible, all available information, a guide manual, or whatever you deem necessary for promotional work in our parish."

Save for the circumstance that it is addressed primarily to priests and educators, this chapter is a partial answer to the foregoing letter. Here are grouped together suggestions that a decade's endeavor in this 'promotional work' have tested over and over. That the several items are taken from the 'case-histories' of parishes in all parts of the country, parishes where Dialog Mass was being started, should give them for our fellow-priests additional cogency and persuasiveness.

The first step towards advancing the day, locally or nationally, when Dialog Mass will be a common-place aspect of Catholicism in this country, is to regard it as a *possible* and *desirable* goal to strive for. "This morning we had a [very complete] *Missa Recitata,*" said Bishop Schlarman to his priests in a sermon on "The Minimum Liturgical Program For a Parish." "While a *Missa Recitata* cannot be considered as something that should be practiced exclusively, there will be few parishes where something like it could not be done." [2]

"We should look forward," says that far-seeing leader, Bishop E. V. O'Hara, to the priests of the Kansas City Diocese, "to have our parish Mass on Sunday conducted in this manner. There is no thought of being hurried in this matter, for haste would probably result in defeating any permanent hope of achievement." To a visitor at a Liturgical Week in Passau it might have seemed superfluous that the Ordinary, the Most Reverend S. C. Landersdorfer, should call a special conference for the clergy, "at which he begged them earnestly *never to speak slightingly* of popular participation in the liturgy, and to introduce the Dialog Mass *uniformly* in all the parishes." [3] The laity can easily gather, from a joking remark, that priests, as a group, are opposed to the introduction of Dialog Mass: witness this passage in a letter written, as it happens, where Dialog Mass is now spreading quite rapidly. As far as it is accurate, it presents a situation wherein the laity are informed that Pope and Archbishop must take their lead from the priest in the parish:

"I waited until I could talk to Father about the *Missa Recitata.* His reply, in brief, was: The Holy Father desires the spread of the Dialog Mass. He

[2] *Catholic Mind*, XXXIII. 6 (March 22, 1935), 118.
[3] Bishop Landersdorfer: cf. *Orate Fratres*, XIV, 4 (February 18, 1940), 184.

therefore supposes that the Archbishop does, too. The majority of the priests with whom Father is acquainted do not favor the Dialog Mass, except for special groups such as the Sodalists. It is impossible, according to them, to teach all the congregation, and therefore those reciting the Mass prove too great a distraction for those unable to do so."

Not to talk slightingly of Dialog Mass is just negative: an early step in positive work on its behalf is for the priest to *let the laity sense and share* his love of holy Mass. "To acquaint us with the richnesses of the Mass," writes a woman from Toledo, "our director gave us a series of studies on the Mass (using charts), which he later extended to talks on the Mystical Body of Christ. To begin with, Father ——— brought to us a love and reverence for the Mass, which we sensed immediately. In saying Mass he maintains a steady pace and his words are well-articulated."

The Reverend Ernest A. Burtle, pastor of 450 souls in Mt. Sterling, Illinois, has described in print how his first efforts in liturgical reform was to imbue his rural flock with a deep love of the Eucharist, especially in holy Mass. The rest, he says, was easy: "Loving the Mass, it was a comparatively easy step to introduce the Dialog Mass; and so low Mass, with server alone responding, is a thing of the past in the parish. All Masses are either high Masses or Dialog Masses. Father Stedman's *My Sunday Missal and Manual* (250 missals are in circulation in the parish [of 450 baptized souls!]), is the text-book for the Dialog Mass. Former altarboys and high school students were urged to brush up on their Latin to form a hurried nucleus for 'putting over' the Dialog Mass, and there are on record several remarkable examples of the swiftness

with which untrained men and women mastered the
'impossible tongue.'"[4]   Loving the Mass made it easy
to do even that!

In the foregoing citation, Father Burtle passed from
the matter of motivation to that of inaugural procedure
and method, and we may well follow his lead.   In the
first place, it must never be lost sight of that it is the
bishop who authorizes the introduction of Dialog
Mass.   This is an official direction given by the Holy
See.[5]   In many American dioceses this permission, as
having been granted in general terms already, is now
presumptive.

Permission secured, the next step is to select a group
among the laity, whose role it will be to form the
nucleus for communal recitation.   The group, if at
all possible, should be provided with a leader.   His
rural situation in Mt. Sterling suggested to Father
Burtle to use former servers and high-school students:
every parish would have some such parishioners.   "I
am going to start with the members of the Holy Name
Society," writes a Staten Island pastor.   "It may interest you to know that as a Sodality project from now
until June . . . [we] are going to exemplify how
to assist at the *Missa Recitata*.   We feel that if we are
able to make this project successful, we shall have
accomplished something very great for the honor and
glory of God," writes a correspondent in the Diocese
of Buffalo.   A further hint with regard to this nucleus-
group, that has often been found helpful, is to 'plant'
small colonies of these trained members here and there
in the church, and encourage the congregation to join
with them in making the responses, and reciting the

---

[4] Cf. *Orate Fratres*, XV, 7 (May 18, 1941), 321-22.
[5] *Acta Apostolicae Sedis*, XIV, 1922, 505: *Decreta Authentica Congregationis Sacrorum Rituum*, No. 4375, Appendix II, 39.

parts of the Mass.   Let the people be urged to say the words very softly at first, and, as they become sure of themselves, to match the key of the nucleus group. "Our leader checks the variable parts of the Mass with Father beforehand for accuracy.   She sits about half-way so that her voice will be heard by all," thus a woman prefect of a Sodality in describing a situation in which no priest or other man is available for the task of leader.

The Reverend William Frawley, Latrobe (Diocese of Pittsburgh), has published a rather full account of how he is using the Sodality in "launching the *Missa Recitata.*"   It will be seen from his account that he went at one leap from silence to a very full form of Dialog Mass, instead of starting with a series of the simplest responses only, as was outlined in the previous chapter.   Also his account was written too soon to be able to reflect the results of the Dialog Mass on the other parishioners.   Despite these drawbacks, the account is a convincing document.

"LAUNCHING THE *MISSA RECITATA*

"Six of my Sodalists and I came away from the Summer School of Catholic Action quite impressed with the Community Mass.   After pro and con discussion we decided to 'take a crack' at it in conjunction with our annual Communion breakfast and reception of candidates.

"At our regular Sodality meeting we issued a call for volunteers who would agree to practice the recited Mass during the month.   (At the meeting we explained just what the Community Mass is, its advantages from the layman's standpoint. . .)

St. Patrick's in Superior Inaugurates Dialog Mass

"We then distributed copies of the *Community Mass* to about twenty-five volunteers. On the following Thursday the first practice session was conducted. I presided at this practice session, for many of the girls had never taken Latin in school. But to offer this, or the fact that Latin is too hard for the girls, is an unfounded objection in most cases. Surely, if a ten year old boy can memorize Latin, a young lady can at least read it in time.

"We went through the Mass that first night about three or four times, very slowly, and practised difficult pronunciations and passages. On the whole, our first attempt was satisfactory. The Sodalists took the copies home with them and promised to report for the other training classes on successive Thursdays throughout the month.

"By enlisting the aid of our probation class (twenty-seven girls about to be received into the Sodality), thereby making the Community Mass an essential part of their training, and by distributing copies to the chairman of the various Committees of the Sodality, the number of those studying the Mass was increased to about one hundred. At the end of the month we all convened in the church where the final practice was held. I directed the girls from the pulpit, while the other curate acted as celebrant.

"Our first Community Mass was offered on Sodality Sunday of the following month. Two hundred copies of the booklet were not enough, for about two hundred and fifty to three hundred girls attended. It is our hope, eventually, to obtain enough books for everyone who attends the Sodality Mass, so that they won't be distracted in their own prayers, and that they may join in reciting the Mass with the Sodalists.

"Everyone was pleased with the Community Mass. We heard many comments about it. We intend to continue our training class and hope for more smoothness and efficiency in succeeding months. I think the idea will spread among the parishioners and that they will want to 'pray the Mass' themselves." [6]

There is a major difficulty involved in the question of the use of the Latin language, however zeal and devotedness may make it look very easy. The problem is not often presented from the angle that proved a matter of scruple to the Fulton Sheen Guild in a Southern city, namely, that the laity are not allowed to recite the Latin! "During the past year," the communication begins, "a few members of the Fulton Sheen Guild have been participating in the *Missa Recitata* on Saturday mornings in a small chapel, where few others are present besides our own group. . . The Spiritual Director of the chapel where we have the Mass suggested that we find out whether or not it is proper for the laity to recite in Latin any of the prayers which are printed in English for recitation by the congregation. [Reference is made to the booklet, *Community Mass*, published by *The Queen's Work*.] We do not understand why these prayers could not properly be said in Latin as well as in English. . . The priest who celebrates the Mass for us is willing and eager for our group to say in Latin as many of the prayers as we are privileged to do. He has found that our saying the prayers aloud does not delay him at any time during the Mass." Not many pastors will be troubled on the score of having groups of the laity able and eager to pray in Latin as much as is allowed. Let them, for their comfort, read Bishop Schlarman's ac-

[6] *Directors' Bulletin*, X, 3 (December, 1940), 1.

count of how Dialog Mass for adults is celebrated in the Peoria Cathedral, and then consult at the end of this chapter the printed form there used: "The 12 o'clock Mass on Sundays in the Cathedral is a *Missa Recitata*. The congregation does not yet respond to the prayers at the foot of the altar. A priest in the pulpit reads the Epistle and Gospel in English while the celebrant reads them at the altar. That gives more time for the sermon. The whole congregation recites the *Credo* in English." A glance now at the form used in Peoria discloses that the responses at this adult Dialog Mass include these: *Kyrie eleison, Christe eleison, Et cum spiritu tuo, Amen, Gloria tibi Domine, Suscipiat . . . , Habemus ad Dominum, Dignum et iustum est, Sed libera nos a malo, Deo gratias, Gloria tibi Domine*: communal recitation in this Peoria form embraces the entire *Sanctus* and the *Agnus Dei* (after the first two words). Only one of these responses exceeds five words in length, and the wording of the short recited parts is familiar *by sound* from its constant occurrence in high Mass. "As yet we have not handled the *Confiteor* or the *Domine non sum dignus* at our Communion," writes a lay correspondent, "but it is our intention eventually to recite these in Latin." The writer has previously broached the question, to the discussion of which Pope Pius XI said he saw no objection whatever, as to whether there may not be in the not too distant future a definite place for the vernacular in our Roman Mass.[7] But meanwhile Dialog Mass must surmount this difficulty of language. Perhaps it will be the instrument used to create the situation where a place for the mother-tongue will seem inevitable. "My opinion, if it is

[7] Cf. *Men*, 237-54.

worth anything," a priest wrote me recently, "is that the vernacular should be used throughout the Mass of the Catechumens, which would include the Creed, though I don't suppose we can expect it to happen in this generation." This furnishes an additional reason for wishing Father B—— long length of days!

This naturally brings us to the consideration of the time element. "The impracticability of it: with all the announcements we have to make . . . it is pretty difficult to complete the Masses on an hourly schedule, which is necessary in order that all the parishioners may be given the opportunity to assist at the holy Sacrifice," such is the wording one priest gives to this very widespread feeling that Dialog Mass entails a decided lengthening of the Mass. "We have our Masses every three-quarters of an hour, and so I don't see what can be done about Dialog Mass, much as I would like to have it in the parish," states another colleague in the ministry. For such simple, short responses as those mentioned in the preceding paragraph, and the very brief recitation, as outlined by Bishop Schlarman, the Mass ought not be delayed more than two or three minutes at the most. The altar-boys must make the responses in any case, and the people beyond the sanctuary rail, especially if a leader keeps them on the *qui vive* and together, can make the short answers with little noticeable delay in the rite. Should there be a momentary slowing of the Mass, would one count it as time lost or as time gained? To quote once from a Toledo correspondent already cited: "In saying Mass he maintains a steady pace and his words are well-articulated. He is so desirous of our participation that he is willing to wait for us, but there is not much delay, possibly a little at the *Munda cor meum* and the

Lavabo. . . Yesterday, the Mass, with the reading of
the Epistle and Gospel, announcements and sermon,
and Communion, took just forty-five minutes." Most
priests will admit that this *confrère* in Toledo manages
an edifying Dialog Mass without breaking up the
three-quarter-hour schedule.

Something that in many places touches the possibility of having Dialog Mass for adults on Sundays is
the distribution of holy Communion — at Communion
time. One recalls in this connection words of wisdom
written by a priest from Rome some years ago: "In
all cases let the liturgical prescriptions for the distribution of Communion be faithfully observed, seeking to
combine (and this can be done with good will), the
good of souls with the decorum which is to be shown
to the Blessed Sacrament. Such combinations as, for
instance, a priest distributing Communion independently of the Mass, and with no regard for the
point at which the sacrificial Action has arrived, with
ceremonies improvised then and there, these cases, I
say, if perchance they may be tolerated on some rare,
extraordinary occasion, must by no means pass into
daily use." The *Rituale Romanum,* revised long after
the restoration of frequent Communion by Pius X,
makes no provision for an almost continuous distribution of Communion during a great part of the Mass:
*Intra Missam autem Communio populi statim post
Communionem celebrantis fieri debet (nisi quandoque
ex rationabili causa proxime ante aut statim post Missam privatam sit facienda), cum Orationes, quae in
Missa post Communionem dicuntur, non solum ad
Sacerdotem, sed etiam ad alios communicantes spec-
tent,"* (*Tit.* IV, 2, 11). In this connection we cite a
second time from that letter evoked by the memories

of the Dialog Mass at Mont-St.-Michel. Here one lay person in writing to another gives in unstudied phrases reasoning that runs exactly parallel to that of the *Rituale Romanum :* the distribution of Communion at other than the Communion time robs the Missal-prayers of their applicability to the lay communicants. The letter :

"Before the happy day arrives, if it *ever* arrives, when I can enjoy such a Mass in the U.S.A., it would be a decided improvement if our priests helped those of us who like to use a missal at Mass by refraining from the distribution of holy Communion *until the Communion time*. I realize that presents obstacles, but hardly insurmountable ones. In my opinion the prayers in the missal preceding the Communion are a most appropriate preparation for the reception of the Sacrament. How can one profitably use a missal when the priest who distributes holy Communion starts to do so before the Consecration?"

The introduction of Dialog Mass in a parish at once raises the question of what a layman called a 'guide manual,' a printed text. At the end of this chapter is appended the form used in Peoria Cathedral, where worshippers find the printed card, six-and three-quarter inches by ten inches in size, awaiting them in the pews. *My Sunday Missal* (Stedman), *Following the Mass* (Glavin), *The Leaflet Missal* (Bussard), and even Carmelite and Dominican Rite missals are now arranged to provide for this congregational recitation in English or Latin or both. Reference was made in the foregoing paragraphs to the booklet, *Community Mass,* arranged by W. H. Puetter, S.J., published by *The Queen's Work.* It has met in recent years with very widespread acceptance. Bishop O'Hara has pre-

scribed it for the CYO of Kansas City; it is the text
of the La Crosse CYO, and the same is true of most of
the places where the Sodalists are the 'shock-troops'
for the inaugural campaign for Dialog Mass.

Answering the laity's objections, that may possibly
attend the beginning of Dialog Mass in a parish, brings
in the personal equation, tact, consideration; but the
difficulties themselves are easily reduced to a few:

"It's not obligatory."	"No, but it is the *better* way. The talking-pictures superseded the silents because they were better."
"It's new, strange, novel."	"That is what our parents said about frequent Communion in 1905."
"It upsets private devotions."	"It builds up communal praying, which our Holy Father says we need just now."
"It invites disorder."	"Common reverence and care obviate this."
"We older people resent it."	"There is still the option of a 'silent' Mass."
"Why make Mass harder?"	"Active participation, the Pope says, makes Mass fuller, richer."

So this little book, undertaken on requests more
than once received, is offered to his fellow-priests and
educators with the hope that it prove helpful to
them in bridging the wide gap between our present
status and that active, conscious co-worship of the laity
with the priest in the joint sharing in the priestly
activity of the great High Priest, Jesus Christ. When
will our twenty-some million Catholics in the pews
pass over, as Pius XI considered so necessary, from the

status of detached and silent spectators, to that of active participants in the Mass, and both by recitation and by song mingle their voices with those of priest and choir? When will our twenty-some million Catholics exert the full pressure of their numbers in the formation and guidance of what is beginning to be called the social conscience of America? Do not these two questions help to answer each other? A non-Catholic country-man, Walter C. Frame, spoke words that are pointed in a recent "Plain Talk to You Catholics." His indictment read in part:

"It may be a sign of rectitude and internal harmony that many of you accept the Mass with the same air of detachment with which one takes setting-up exercises in the morning. Remember, I am a Protestant, trained in a Puritan environment, and I am expressing the prejudices of my kind. When Mass is repeated several times in a morning, I can find no excuse for entering late. In any Protestant church of my acquaintance, such conduct would be inexcusable; yet such scenes do occur in Catholic services. Granted that this has nothing to do with the inner light, yet the impression created can be deplorable.

"As a Protestant I cannot understand or forgive a careless performance of the Mass. . . The sad truth is that it is not said well in too many places. It is not even muttered. It is mumbled. The attitude seems to be that it is 'patter — not generally heard and if it is, it does not matter.' The point is that it *does* matter. (It may not matter to a Catholic whose attention is trained on the Eucharist, and not upon its evocation.) You Catholics have a service which is part of the river of consciousness flowing from the remote past into the present. You have a beautiful ritual which forms a setting for your belief as a jeweled monstrance holds the Host. If you wish others to respect and revere that belief, you should not neglect the color, the moving beauty of the Mass." [8]

If this writer had understood, however vaguely, that sacrifice is the highest expression of religion, or that assisting at the Mass, as Trent said, is *the holiest thing the faithful can do,* would he not feel much more disturbed than he now confesses to be? Where are the 'cold' Catholics he has seen in our churches to acquire the new fire that will set them alight and aflame to be the light of the world amid the fast-gathering, all-embracing gloom? "The faithful come to church," said Pius XI in *Divini cultus sanctitatem,* "to derive piety from its chief source, by taking an active part in the venerated mysteries and the public, solemn prayers of the Church."

[8] Cf. *America,* LXIII, 8 (June 1, 1940), 203.

APPENDIX

FORM OF DIALOG MASS, ST. MARY'S CATHEDRAL, PEORIA [Front]

"Our most ardent desire being that the true Christian spirit flourish again, it is necessary to provide that . . . the faithful . . . find this spirit at its primary source, which is the **active participation** in the public and solemn prayers of the Church." **Pope Pius X.**

After the Introit, the Celebrant returns to the center of the Altar:

Celebrant: Kyrie eleison.

All answer: Kyrie eleison.

Celebrant: Kyrie eleison.

All answer: Christe eleison.

Celebrant: Christe eleison.

All answer: Christe eleison.

Celebrant: Kyrie eleison.

All answer: Kyrie eleison.

Celebrant: Kyrie eleison.

Celebrant then turns toward the people:

Celebrant: Dominus vobiscum.

All answer: Et cum spiritu tuo.

Celebrant returns to the Epistle side of Altar. Here he concludes each of the Orations by saying:

Celebrant: Per omnia saecula saeculorum.

All answer: Amen.

When Celebrant begins the Gospel, he says:

Celebrant: Dominus vobiscum.

All answer: Et cum spiritu tuo.

Celebrant: Sequentia sancti Evangelii secundum Matthaeum.

All answer: Gloria tibi, Domine.

After saying the Creed, the Celebrant turns toward the people and says:

Celebrant: Dominus vobiscum.

All answer: Et cum spiritu tuo.

After washing his hands, the Celebrant returns to the center of the Altar, and turning toward the people, says:

Celebrant: Orate Fratres.

All answer: Suscipiat Dominus / sacrificium de manibus tuis / ad laudem et gloriam nominis sui / ad utilitatem quoque nostram / totiusque Ecclesiae suae sanctae.

The Celebrant begins the Preface by saying:

Celebrant: Per omnia saecula saeculorum.

All answer: Amen.

Celebrant: Dominus vobiscum.

All answer: Et cum spiritu tuo.

Celebrant: Sursum corda.

All answer: Habemus ad Dominum.

Celebrant: Gratias agamus Domino Deo nostro.

All answer: Dignum et iustum est.

At the end of the Preface, **all recite the Sanctus with the Celebrant:**

Sanctus / Sanctus / Sanctus / Dominus Deus Sabaoth / Pleni sunt caeli et terra gloria tua. / Hosanna in excelsis. / Benedictus qui venit in nomine Domini. / Hosanna in excelsis.

After the Consecration, the Celebrant begins the Pater Noster by saying:

Celebrant: Per omnia saecula saeculorum.

All answer: Amen.

The Celebrant ends the Pater Noster by saying:

Celebrant: Et ne nos inducas in tentationem.

All answer: Sed libera nos a malo.

After a short prayer, the Celebrant continues:

Celebrant: Per omnia saecula saeculorum.

All answer: Amen.

Celebrant: Pax Domini sit semper vobiscum.

All answer: Et cum spiritu tuo.

The Celebrant now says the Agnus Dei. As soon as he has said the first two words, **all say the Agnus Dei with him.**

Celebrant: Agnus Dei —

All answer: —qui tollis peccata mundi. / Miserere nobis. / Agnus Dei, / qui tollis peccata mundi. / Miserere nobis. / Agnus Dei, / qui tollis peccata mundi. / Dona nobis pacem.

After the chalice has been covered, the Celebrant goes to the Epistle side of the Altar and recites the Communion Antiphon. He returns to the center of the Altar, turns toward the people and says:

Celebrant: Dominus vobiscum.

All answer: Et cum spiritu tuo.

The Celebrant goes to the Epistle side of the Altar and concludes each of the Post-Communion prayers by saying:

Celebrant: Per omnia saecula saeculorum.

All answer: Amen.

The Celebrant returns to the center of the Altar, turns to the people and says:

Celebrant: Dominus vobiscum.

All answer: Et cum spiritu tuo.

Celebrant: Ite, Missa est.   (Or Benedicamus Domino)

All answer: Deo gratias.

The Celebrant then gives the Blessing by saying:

Celebrant: Benedicat vos, Omnipotens Deus, Pater et Filius, et Spiritus Sanctus.

All answer: Amen.

The Celebrant begins the Last Gospel by saying:

Celebrant: Dominus vobiscum.

All answer: Et cum spiritu tuo.

Celebrant: Initium sancti Evangelii secundum Ioannem.

All answer: Gloria tibi, Domine.

INDEX

INDEX

213

Fontbonne College (St. Louis), 126.
Forbes, Archbishop W. (Ottawa), 65.
Fordham University (New York), 126.
Forest Park, Ill., 157.
Forster, Rev. F., 137.
Fort Devens, Mass., 100.
Fort Dodge, Ia., 107.
Fort Wayne, Ind., 93, 104, 105.
Fox, Monsignor E., 155.
Frame, Rev. W. C., 204, 205.
Franch, P.SS.C., Rev. B., 158.
Franklin Park, Ill., 157.
Frawley, Monsignor D., 152.
Frawley, Rev. William, 196.
Frederick the Great, 39.
Fremont, Ohio, 105.
Fremont Park, Ill., 157.
Frisch, Rev. A., 134.
Fulton Sheen Guild, 198.

Galena, Kas., 120.
Galesburg, Ill., 103.
Gallery, Rev. J. I., 158.
Galloway, Wis., 135.
Gallup, N. M., 125.
Galveston, Tex., 123.
Gamble, C.PP.S., Rev., A. V., 51.
Geneva, Wis., 135.
Genoa (Italy), 54, 60, 61, 63, 69, 80.
Genzan (Chosen), 83.
Georgetown, D. C., 98.
Georgetown University (Washington), 126.
Georgiaville, R. I., 101.
Geoville, Kas., 117.
Gerken, Archbishop (Santa Fe), R., 125.
Gerow, Bishop R. O. (Natchez), xii.
Geschichte der Päpste (Pastor), 38, 39.
Giambastiani, O.S.M., Rev. L., 154.
Gille, Rev. C. W., 134.
Gillespie, Rev. F. J., 155.
Glavin, Monsignor J. F., 202.
Glen Ellyn, Ill., 157.
Gniesen-Posen (Poland), 77.
Gomá y Tomás, I, Cardinal Archbishop (Toledo), 79.
Graf, C.PP.S., Rev. J., 137.
Grand Forks, N. D., 122.
Grand Island, Nebr., 107.
Grand Rapids, Mich., 106.
Gray, Rev. F. X., 136.

Great Bend, Kas., 120.
Great Falls, Mont., 82.
Green Bay, Wis., 109.
Greenwich (Jamaica), 67.
Greenwood, Wis., 135.
Gregorian Chant, for sake of Christian spirit, 13; must be given to people (Pius X), 40; restoration resisted, 12, 13.
Gregory the Great, St. *Epis. IX*, 25.
Grembowicz, Rev. J. A., 157.
Gretna, La., 111.
Griffin, Rev. W. R., Auxiliary Bishop (La Crosse), 89, 110, 130.
Gronkowski, Rev. C. I., 150.
Guilfoyle, Bishop R. (Altoona), 114.
Gurk-Klagenfurt, Synod, 76.

Haas, Rev. M., 136.
Hackner, Rev. W. T., 135.
Haines, Rev. C. W., 135.
Hanssens, S.J., Rev. I. M., 49, 50, 51, 54, 55.
Hardy, Rev. G. R., 137.
Harrisburg, Pa., 115.
Hartford, Conn., 100.
Hartington, Nebr., 107.
Hartnett, D., 150.
Harvey, Ill., 157.
Hauck, Monsignor J. B., 137.
Hayes, Rev. P. J., 155.
Hayes, Rev. T. J., 154.
Hays, Kas., 117, 127.
Helena, Mont., 116.
Helletsville, Tex., 123.
d'Herbigny, S.J., Bishop M., 57, 58.
Hewitt, Wis., 135.
Highland Park, Ill., 157.
Hillenbrand, Rev. F. E., 156.
Hillsboro, Wis., 135.
Hinsley, A. Cardinal Archbishop (Westminster), 64, 71, 72.
Hippolytus, St., *Apostolic Tradition*, 27.
Hiroshima (Japan), 83.
Hishen, Rev. J. D., 152.
Hiti, Rev. M. J., 159.
Hlond, A., Cardinal Archbishop (Gniesen-Posen), 77.
Hoffmann, Rev. A. A., 136.
Hoffmann, Rev. H. J., 137.
Hokah, Minn., 123.
Holy Cross, Ind., 127.
Holy Cross (Jamaica), 67.